THE ADDERALL EMPIRE

THE
ADDERALL
EMPIRE
A Life With ADHD and the Millennials' Drug of Choice

Andrew K. Smith

NEW YORK

THE ADDERALL EMPIRE

A Life With ADHD and the Millennials' Drug of Choice

© 2014 Andrew K. Smith.

Published in New York, New York, by Morgan James Publishing. Morgan James and The Entrepreneurial Publisher are trademarks of Morgan James, LLC. www.MorganJamesPublishing.com

The Morgan James Speakers Group can bring authors to your live event. For more information or to book an event visit The Morgan James Speakers Group at www.TheMorganJamesSpeakersGroup.com.

FREE eBook edition for your existing eReader with purchase

_____

PRINT NAME ABOVE

For more information, instructions, restrictions, and to register your copy, go to **www.bitlit.ca/readers/register** or use your QR Reader to scan the barcode:

ISBN 978-1-61448-892-7 paperback
ISBN 978-1-61448-893-4 eBook
ISBN 978-1-61448-894-1 audio
ISBN 978-1-61448-895-8 hardcover
Library of Congress Control Number:
2013955199

Front Cover Design by:
Brian Matthew Chinn
brianmchinn@gmail.com

Cover Design by:
Chris Treccani
www.3dogdesign.net

Interior Design by:
Bonnie Bushman
bonnie@caboodlegraphics.com

In an effort to support local communities, raise awareness and funds, Morgan James Publishing donates a percentage of all book sales for the life of each book to Habitat for Humanity Peninsula and Greater Williamsburg.

Get involved today, visit
www.MorganJamesBuilds.com

Dear Mom & Dad,
This Book Is For You

Author's Note:

My true-to-life name is Andrew K. Smith. The incidents described in this book are genuine to the best of my memory, though certain time periods, characters, whereabouts, and other frivolous elements have been reformed to safeguard the innocent.

Please be advised that I wrote this book not for me, but for the readers. I wrote it not only to rejuvenate awareness of ADHD, but to bring into society a more complete view of the effects Adderall can have on a life.

"Here's to the crazy ones, the misfits, the rebels, the troublemakers, the round pegs in the square holes…the ones who see things differently—they're not fond of rules…You can quote them, disagree with them, glorify or vilify them, but the only thing you can't do is ignore them because they change things…they push the human race forward, and while some may see them as the crazy ones, we see genius, because the ones who are crazy enough to think that they can change the world, are the ones who do."

—Steve Jobs

CONTENTS

Inside the Adderall Empire
FRAGMENT ONE

Those first few sunbreaks are spellbinding, flooded with hyper awareness. I see gold grass, clear diamonds. I smile, and smile again. I begin to realize that, like Lewis and Clark, I might need a compass, something to point me in the right direction. But when it comes to decrypting well-being, as opposed to a whole geographic region, there is little support.

So as the sun comes up in Edmonds, Washington, I lie on my hand-me-down mattress inspecting the quick, morning sun sparkling on my pill canteen. No matter what is happening in that room, I know my pills are watching me. The pills glare out of the bottle: a light-carrot orange, oblong, diamond capsule. Quickly put together, small and lightweight, with a panicky, smooth, plastic-like crust.

But there is something about the way the small orange beads are still, something scornful and knowing that tells me that somewhere below this restless sturdiness is a flaw as infinite as it is inflexible, like an ex-girlfriend's hazardous rage.

Swiftly I turn to face the bottle, as though God's hand came down to Earth and slapped me in the face, turning my life around. The house is blackening. The bottle stands on my nightstand at my service. I am terribly aware of the pills' muscles, and of mine. I get up and walk over to the nightstand and stick my tongue out at it. I want to stand here, concealed and still. But then, far inside, I feel the chemical bond of amphetamines scrambling to help improve my well-being, gushing to unclutter the gates of the synthetically built empire and let the noble archduke of delight come in.

I feel aimless, like a ball, bouncing and bouncing, and I begin to wonder where I'll land: Somewhere in the Adderall Empire.

All the years of being the kid who parents told their sons and daughters not to hang out with—all those times I embarrassed my family and myself—were over. My main fear was that I would end up in jail or become that crazy guy everyone avoids in town. So when those cops took the handcuffs off me during my freshman year of high school, my parents got me some assistance.

My life changed when I was diagnosed with ADHD. I was prescribed Adderall and entered the Adderall Empire.

PART I

PRE-DIAGNOSIS

CHAPTER ONE

STREAKING

Occurred: Autumn 2005

The real turning point happened when I was fifteen years old. The night before I decided to go streaking, it was noisy and lavish at my curly-haired friend Chester's house on Pine Street. A few cohorts and I slumped on the couch, watching Will Ferrell "streak through the quad" in the movie *Old School*.

It inspired me. I thought about how liberating it would feel to expose myself for the public laughs of my entourage. I voiced my thoughts, considering it harmless, even kind, to pull the stunt. So I pinkie promised everyone in the room: At the next football game, at half-time, I would streak.

Earlier that year I had transferred from Archbishop Murphy High School, a private school with four hundred students, to Edmonds Woodway High School, a public school with two thousand students. I had already found a circle of friends who accepted me, but I wanted to be *popular*. I also wanted to feel free and to rebel against society. Most of all, though, I wanted to make people laugh. I was a fiend for laughs—no heed to the consequence—and that desire always seemed to get me into trouble.

It was the middle of October. Wet leaves stuck to the streets and a buzz began to spread through town that something was about to go down. Nobody could quite pinpoint it—except for my friends.

When I woke up on Friday, my thoughts were doing jumping jacks off the walls of my brain. I was anxious from head to toe. My feelings about the stunt were sprinkled with both triumph and guilt. I loved my friends and I had to be a man of my word. These were neighbors, friends I'd grown up with and was becoming a man with. They were my biggest fans. But I couldn't completely quell the thoughts of possible repercussions.

Before any of this naked business could go down, I found a pair of scissors and did some manscaping. Not that I was self-conscious or anything, but I wanted to appear as big as possible. If I was going to follow through, I was going to do it in style. After a few clips, I looked at myself in the mirror. My reflection muttered a short pep talk—"You can do this, Andrew. You the man."

I got dressed and cleaned the smudges of dirt off my white high-top Reeboks. I skipped breakfast and scurried out the door, catching the Community Transit bus 110 to school.

The air outside was brisk, and I turned the dial of my creative jetpacks to full blast. I tried to cook up a strategy from scratch during the ride to school. More than anything else, I did not want to get caught.

When the school day was over, I went to football practice. I had recently joined the team and practice was held in the outfield of the baseball field. My mind buzzed with strategies—not football strategies—and I noticed that the baseball field was directly to the left side of the end zone of the football stadium. With a mental note about the fence saved for that night, I tried to focus on my tackles.

All my ducks were in a row by six that night, and I was determined to pull off this wild feat. There was an hour and a half before the game started and a few teammates were walking to Burger King for dinner. While we ate I realized that I needed something to cover my face, as getting caught was something I did not want to happen. The creative jetpacks in my mind turned on again, and it came to me: I would use the brown Burger King bag as my mask. One of my teammates had a roll of scotch tape and scissors in his backpack. Fate had given me the tools to pull this off.

Before leaving Burger King, I cut two eyeholes in the front of the bag and a slit slightly up the backside for slack. The guys giggled as I modeled the bag over my head, and I knew I was ready. We walked back across the street toward the stadium.

Moments later we arrived at the gate entrance, where I said goodbyes to my teammates. They all thought I was going to chicken out. I sat on a bench outside the gate for a few moments, my heart pounding like the pistons of an engine and my thoughts twirling in figure eights.

You can do this. You can do this, I thought. I stood up and casually walked over to the baseball field. As I passed the bleachers by the clubhouse, I saw a bald-headed African-American man talking to himself in the bleachers. He might have been a dad of one of the players on the team.

Edmonds Woodway was playing against Shorecrest. Both teams were 7-0, and people had poured into the stadium like it was a bum rush for the concessions stand at a Seahawks game.

I managed to sneak past the man without a stop and chat, and scooted into the grass alley behind the clubhouse next to the fence. Sitting, leaning with my back against the side of the clubhouse, I waited. The supplies were in my front sweatshirt pocket. I had two painful quarters to build up my courage and, while I sat there, I realized I had no exit route. If I can just make it to the other end zone, I thought, I'll know what to do. Then I'll come back for my clothes afterward.

Every minute felt like a millennium. Finally the half-time horn blared and the players ran into the tunnel that led to the locker rooms under the stadium. As the cheerleader drill team came out and started its routine, I said quietly, "Here I go," and peeled off my sweatshirt and plain white t-shirt, my shoes, my jeans, my boxers, and my socks. I put back on my high-tops. I jumped up and down a couple of times to get fired up. I was nervous and the beverage I had at Burger King had run right through me. I had to pee so I walked over and sprayed the metal fence as a gust of wind blew in between my legs. It was getting colder.

When I shook off and turned around, the wind had carried my paper bag mask out of my sweatshirt and blown it against the side of the clubhouse. I bolted to it as another gust blew it further, this time around the side of the clubhouse. "FFFffffff----!" I yelled, still standing nude. I took off my shoes and put my pants, shoes, and sweatshirt on. I chased after the bag. Finally I caught up with the bag floating toward the bleachers where the man was standing. I snatched it with both hands and looked up.

"You watching the game over there, man?" A concerned look smeared his face.

"Yeah uhhh, sorry, you'll see!" I hightailed it back to the alley, skidding on the gravel beneath me.

I ripped off my clothes faster than a teen about to have sex for the first time. I retied my shoes, grabbed the paper bag and stuck it over my head, snatched the tape, peeled a piece, and slapped it on the backside of the bag for support.

Moments later, I ran at full speed toward the fence, like Flash Buddy. A second passed, I put my right arm on the top of the fence and hoisted myself up and over. I was sailing through the air, adrenaline rushing through my loins.

Boom! I landed on the other side and sprinted as fast as I could.

Seconds later I crossed the track that surrounded the field. My head was buzzing. Then I raced through the end zone, past the goalposts, and pumped my fists in the air, screaming, "WOOOOOO!"

I looked to my right and saw blurry dots of color, an audience of over two thousand people. Still running at full speed, I heard muffled sounds from the stands but couldn't clearly make out a single one as I hummed past the 10-yard line.

My heart felt like it was beating outside my chest and I pushed forward, running like Forrest Gump. My muscles were starting to burn. I made it to about the 30-yard line and threw my fists up in the air like I'd won a marathon. As I was approaching the 50-yard line, my inner demons suddenly kicked in. Don't get caught! I felt the need to abort my goal of making it to the other end zone and my legs followed a quick decision to turn around, retreat, head back the way I'd come.

Everything was happening all at once. I returned to the fence and jumped, no hands on the fence. I leaped through the air over the fence and landed roughly, my left shoulder smashing against the side of the clubhouse. My thoughts were jumbled. I ripped the paper bag off my face and squished it down on my clothes, swooped them up, and ran around the side of the fence. The bald man who'd been talking to himself was gone. Oh no, I thought.

My feet carried me to the baseball field and into the dugout where I frantically put my clothes on—faster than an actor in a play. In my panic I forgot to put my shirt on, so I shoved it down my pants. My phone was vibrating. I saw a trash can in the dugout. I might be able to fit in that, I thought. But it was too late. I glanced out of the dugout to confirm the sound of four pounding feet approaching from right field.

I'm screwed.

I sat down and tried to act casual.

One officer came in through the left side of the dugout and another through the right. I was trapped. The cop on the right wheezed, "You're under arrest," dusting the air and his mustache with spit.

I stood up, put my hands in the air. "Okay, okay, you caught me," I muttered.

The cop on the left grabbed my left hand and put it down to my left side, reaching for his handcuffs.

"Excuse me officer, can I take my shirt out? It's in the front of my jeans."

The mustached cop laughed and wheezed. "You may."

I reached down and pulled it out. The other cop, a big-boned guy with dark eyes, plucked the shirt from me and said into his walky-talky, "The streaker must have shaved his pubes!"

I wiggled my eyes, confused. Were they joking around? He gave the shirt a shake and tossed it back. After I scrambled into the armholes, Officer Mustache took my other arm and clicked on the cold metal handcuffs.

"Do you know where you're going, kid?"

"No, where?"

The tall cop glowered at me from under his cap. "You're going to juvenile hall." He paused. "Do you know how many laws your broke? You broke seven."

Officer Mustache seemed to have caught his breath. "We're going to read you your rights now," he piped. Removing a laminated card from his pocket, he read, "You are under arrest for indecent exposure, public nudity, disorderly conduct, public nuisance, disturbing the peace, criminal trespassing, interfering in a sporting game. You have the right to remain silent and refuse to answer questions. Do you understand?"

"Yes," I sulked.

"Anything you do or say may be used against you in a court of law. Do you understand?"

"Yes."

"You have the right to consult an attorney before speaking to the police and to have an attorney present during questioning now or in the future. Do you understand?"

"Yes."

"If you cannot afford an attorney, one will be appointed for you before any questioning if you wish. Do you understand?"

"Yes."

"If you decide to answer questions now without an attorney present you will still have the right to stop answering at any time until you talk to an attorney. Do you understand?"

"Yes."

"Knowing and understanding your rights as I have explained them to you, are you willing to answer my questions without an attorney present?"

"Yes."

"Okay. Let's go." He yanked me out of the dugout like his Siamese twin.

We walked to home plate. Another cop jogged toward us, his glasses bouncing on his face. He stuck out his hand in a STOP gesture.

"Hold on a minute," he said. "He is a student at Woodway. Take him out of those cuffs. The school wants to handle this situation."

My stomach lifted. I was shocked, but I wasn't sure if my new situation was better or worse. The two officers removed the handcuffs and handed me off to the third cop, who grabbed me by my arm and walked toward the front of the school.

"Why did you do it?" he asked.

My heart was pounding a million miles a minute. "I, I…it was a bet!"

"What were you thinking?" He sounded skeptical, and something else. Amused? "I spoke with your principal," he said. "We called your parents to come pick you up, but on Monday you have a meeting with the dean. To discuss your punishment."

"Okay," I sputtered. I was free for now, but I cringed at the thought of my parents having to leave my brother's football game to collect their disorderly son.

Their drive from Archbishop Murphy took almost an hour, during which time I sat on my uncuffed hands under the watch of the myopic police officer. The game ended. By the whoops of the home fans it sounded like a win. The assembly crunched through the gravel lot and slammed car doors. I tried to mull over what I would say to my parents, but my blood was still pumping and it seemed difficult to focus on remorse. I felt…alive.

Our Chevy Suburban pulled through the gravel to where the officer and I sat. My frowning father rolled down the passenger window.

"Get in."

He and my mom jerked their heads to face me as I slid into the back seat. "Phone," mom stated, matter-of-factly. "You're grounded indefinitely."

Tension in the car was high. My dad kept muttering things to himself and my mom kept asking him, "What?" They both angrily shook their heads. They barked half-formed questions at me, interrupting each other. Their questions felt like bullets, yet I had to fight for composure to keep from laughing.

That weekend I was trapped in my room, staring at the clock, waiting for dinner. My phone was hidden somewhere so I couldn't communicate with my friends and ask them what happened in the stands. I punched my pillow over and over again. I curled into a ball and growled in anger.

Prior to dinner I heard someone knock on the front door. I crept out my room and snuck down the hallway with my back against the wall like an FBI agent.

"Hey, we were going for a walk with our dog. How's Andrew doing?"

"Come on in," my dad said.

I recognized the voices of my friend William's parents. They entered and sat at the table. Their distorted voices echoed down the stairway into the holes of my ears. I caught laughter. One of the parents said, "We heard about Andrew streaking—how hilarious. We can totally see Andrew doing it."

"We couldn't—we don't…understand why he did it. We just feel bad for him because now he has to face the consequences coming forth Monday."

That was enough eavesdropping for me, so I tiptoed back to my room and was happy my bud's family was accepting and thought it was funny. I squeezed my eyelids shut and thought again about what I had done. For the first time I felt embarrassed that everyone had seen me naked.

At dinner I was shy and worried about what I had done. I slowly slung some spaghetti on to my plate and slurped it into my mouth. Both my parents were looking at me. My brothers were smiling at me.

After the weekend, I returned to school and found my books for first period in my car. Walking to my first class I caught snickers and bits of conversations—"streaker"—"...front of the entire school..."—"...heard it was a bet..."

William and Jeremy said, "We give you three and a half cool points."

Half an hour into English that morning, there was a knock on the door. The bespectacled officer poked his head through and said, "Andrew, I need to see you." Everyone in the class giggled knowingly. Their reactions puffed up my chest and fueled my ego. I felt like the king of the world as I picked up my books and left the room.

The officer escorted me past the receptionist to the dean's office. The name "Louie Swift" gleamed in etched letters on the gold nameplate on his door, which swung open to the man himself. He sat at his mahogany desk looking at a file, a disturbed look splashed on his face. I sat down and the officer stood behind me. The dean was clean-shaven. He tightened his matte black tie.

"Hello again, Mr. Smith."

"Good morning Mr. Swift."

He glanced back down at the file. "I've been reading about your stunt at the football game. Would you mind explaining to me why you did it?"

"It was a bet," I said lamely, "something I guess I always wanted to do."

His gaze was heavy. My palms were sweaty, so I sat on them. "Look Andrew, I personally don't have too much of a problem with this sort of thing. But my daughter was there—she's only eight years old, you know. Students' parents are sending me angry messages. I have to do something. We can't have another incident like this. There might be copy cats, understand?"

I put my hands in my sweaty palms for a second, and then looked up at the eyes under his knitted brow. "Okay, I understand," I mumbled.

He let my response hang in the air for a moment. "So here is the deal. You are not setting a good example for the other students. I am suspending you from school for two days, starting today. And, you're forbidden from attending any sporting events in the district or surrounding districts, plus extracurricular activities of any kind. That means no school dances. I hope you didn't have a date for homecoming."

"I understand," I repeated in a grunt.

He picked up his phone and asked the secretary for my dad's work phone. A few cordial but stern words had my dad leaving his downtown office by the ferry to pick me up.

My mother came home on her lunch break to put me to work. She's very caring in her role as a nurse, but terrifying when she gets angry. Shoving a broom in one hand and Windex in the other, she made it clear that I would not be on the sofa all day watching television.

CHAPTER TWO

TOSSING KITTENS
Occurred: 1990 to 1996

---

can't remember what I learned first, how to tie my shoes, or how to talk my way out of trouble. In my later years, I took up a *method* I like to call "Keep your mouth shut." Talking my way *into* trouble had turned into too likely an outcome.

My mother said I came out of the womb talking. There I was, all blonde and bloody, six pounds of matter swinging in her arms. Then came the time to pick my name, my destined name. At the time, they looked to my older brother, Griffey, for an answer. He said, "Andrew," and it became a coin toss between Andrew and Rupert. I guess I don't have to tell you what won.

That was how Andrew Kenneth Smith was born. The date was June 6, 1990, the same day as the Normandy landings in 1944, now called D-Day. I don't mean I'm a believer in destiny or irony or anything like that, but sometimes I am inclined to believe. My grandfather, Buddy Smith, was born just blocks from me and he was supposed to go to Normandy, but his baseball coach made sure he went into the Coast Guard instead. If it were not for that baseball coach, I would not be blessed with the power of life because my grandfather most likely would have been blasted into the darkness of the crimson-stained sand on that day in history.

I was raised in the suburbs of Edmonds, Washington, just a short ferry ride from Seattle. My father, Lenny, was a tenacious Certified Public Accountant with a prominent brow ridge and thin light hair—I am a splitting image of his Norwegian appearance. He always wore suits and would sometimes let me pick out the tie he wore for the day. My favorite was the one that would sing the Washington State University song when you squeezed the bottom:

Fight, fight, fight for Washington State!
Win the victory,
Win the day for Crimson and Gray!
Best in the West
We know you'll all do your best,
So on, on, on, on!
Fight to the end!
Honor and glory you must win!
So fight, fight, fight for Washington State and Victory!
"All Hail to Washington State"

It took me a while to learn all the words but you can never start too early on recruiting potential students.

My mother, Pearl, was a registered nurse with blonde hair and tanned German skin. Her voice was so soft, so honeyed that it would touch the back of your soul. But she sometimes competed with me to be the family's most rapid-fire talker. She worked nights, and my dad worked days. Sometimes they even worked at the same time, and for these occasions my brothers and I had a nanny.

We lived on Spruce Street at the top of the hill with all the mailboxes aligned in a row outside our house. Through the kitchen window you could see the long, tall evergreen trees shadowing our house.

I was the youngest of three brothers. Ron, the middle brother with hair as blonde as sand, was always wrestling me in the living room. Griffey was the oldest. The three of us were like peas in a pod, chasing and tripping through the trials of life.

It's hard to remember back to my first years as a troublemaker, but I do remember the day my mother busted out the front door, down the driveway, and chucked my milk bottle into the garbage truck. I was about four years old and I suppose she concluded that I'd exceeded my allotted bottle period, if there was such a thing.

But she had to wait until the garbage man came. She attempted to throw it away in the evening, but I snuck out and stole it out of the garbage can late that rainy night. That created a dramatic situation in the morning: mom furiously yanking the bottle from my grip upon discovering she'd been defied and outsmarted by her four-year-old, waiting until she heard the garbage truck growl up the hill, running out the front door and down the front steps to the end of the driveway, and flinging the bottle at the back of the garbage truck as I howled in protest.

I had made it to the door just in time to watch the bottle's last twirl before it landed in the putrid crevice of the waste truck. I ran down to my room. Had she thrown it away when I was younger, I would not have known to care as much. But I sobbed my eyes out that morning.

Eventually I realized that drinking out of a cup was more efficient.

I am not sure if it was the premature exposures I gained from having older brothers, the shrill demons inside me, or my snappish attention span of a gnat, but early on I began to get a bit of a Machiavellian reputation. My brother Griffey, a tall and skinny fellow with fire-red hair, had a rare set of baseball cards organized in a folder. At age five, during my first year in preschool, my frustrated little soul was acting up. I was mad at him for one reason or another, so early one fall morning I crept into his bedroom and snatched his baseball cards. Mint condition rookie cards of Ken Griffey, Jr., Alex Rodriguez, Randy Johnson, and others. I was dangerously quiet, and like a slithering snake I managed to escape from his room with the prized cards. Then I snuck out the front door and plopped them into the garbage bin right before the garbage man arrived.

My mother woke up just afterward and started preparing breakfast. She looked at me and caught me with a guilty look. Or maybe it was a satisfied look. She always seemed to know. She interrogated me, but by the time I confessed, the garbage man had taken the cards.

When my brother woke up he noticed their absence and came running up the stairs. My mother explained to him what I had done, and he was furious. Furious and devastated. That was the first time I remember feeling misery, anger, and disappointment in myself. But I was still somehow unaware of the harm I had caused. I lost the trust of my oldest brother at age of five. And my parents' hearts were shattering for me.

Losing trust and then slowly climbing back up the ladder to an equilibrium of trust would become all too familiar to me. The top of the ladder was always followed by another mistake, more trouble, and another fall. Soon, the trouble began to come in waves.

After a year of preschool I resisted kindergarten. I refused to go, dug my heels straight into the ground. My mother said I just wanted to be with her, to go shopping with her, that I enjoyed being attached to her at the hip. So I attended another year of preschool.

I stole for the first time before my sixth birthday. I am not sure of the normality of that—young kids stealing—but even now I feel a twinge of remorse. My mother, again, took note of the guilt in my posture one winter day during my second year of preschool. She asked me what was wrong, and I caved. I had taken some Legos from the Lego bin at school, I said. Naturally she got mad at me. The trust was lowering again and I returned the Legos the next day and apologized to my teacher. Thankfully, kids don't get suspended in preschool.

Later that the spring our family cat Charlotte mated with our cousins' cat Bandit and had a litter of kittens. They were beautiful baby kittens, jovial balls of fluff playing around the house.

Unfortunately I had recently heard that cats always land on their feet.

One day my cousins and I were on the second-floor deck of my house. My middle brother Ron was watching me like a hawk from inside. Ron's light hair matched my father's, and we called him Bam Bam because he was the destroyer of toys. On the deck, I bent down and picked up one of the newborn kittens and hurled the small fluff ball off the deck and watched it soar through the air. I guess I was testing the newly-discovered hypothesis. Sure it was a cruel thing to do, but I really didn't know any better.

After I watched the first kitten twirl down to the ground and stick the landing, I chased after the second kitten. Its mother, Charlotte, came running after me as I grabbed her newborn. The second kitten flew airborne across the railing and I peaked over the railing with my chin, watching with eyes bigger than saucers. Charlotte caught up to me and leaped off of the deck after her newborns while my mother and brother came running after me. All three cats landed safely. I was smiling until my mother arrived and put me on restriction. Bam Bam was angry with me for almost killing the family cats.

I never really thought things through until the damage was done. I guess my gnat-like attention span blocked any consideration or fear of consequences. Complete thoughts were rare accomplishments fighting for ground in my hyper-distracted brain.

Then there was the whole sucking the thumb fiasco. I sucked my thumb, secretly in my leisure time, until I was ten. One moment is forever ingrained, hung on a wall in my downstairs hallway. It's a picture drawn by an artist, one of each of my brothers and me. I would not take it out of my mouth so he drew my palm clinched with my thumb pointing in between my lips, being sucked like a vacuum, with my two brothers at my side, smiling with their buck teeth.

I thought this was a sign, a sign from some spirit, smashing the meaning of my accidental witty, stubborn, attachment towards life. Sucking my thumb was a metaphor for my life. I clamp on to the people I meet and embrace the saps from my heart.

After my second preschool year ended, my mother made it clear that I had to go to kindergarten. As a six-year-old going on seven, I would be the oldest kid in class. There are always the old ones and the young ones in class, and I think being at either end of the age spectrum affects a person's overall experience in school. Being on the older end of the spectrum placed me in a leadership position. I was also taller than all of my classmates, which gave me a sense of dominance and power each year of school, until I stopped growing.

My parents were doing well enough in their careers to allow my brothers and me to attend private school. All three of us were placed in a school called Holy Rosary. When I got there I had to wear a uniform: blue corduroys, white shirt, and a blue V-neck sweater. We all looked identical in formation as we traveled the halls. The girls wore similar blue vests, but instead of pants they wore plaid red and blue skirts. I never liked those uniforms. I wanted to be different, and my gentle eccentricities were constantly trying to bust out of the confines of those damn sweaters.

My kindergarten teacher, Mrs. Essex, and me.

Mrs. Essex was my kindergarten teacher—a short older lady with black hair that was beginning to tinge with gray. She was kind and always had the greatest Show and Tell expos in her class. Kindergarten was probably the only year of school that I behaved well. There were exceptions though, and they always seemed to have to do with my propensity for strong displays of sexuality.

Inside The Adderall Empire
FRAGMENT TWO

ADHD is a bursting galactic star that crisscrosses inside the walls of your mind and twinkles—ripping your focus into several pieces. Then you are left picking up the pieces after the galactic star treats your thought process like a playground.

I'd say the ADHD-free version of me would be clear as glass, and I could look in the mirror long enough to look myself in the eyes. ADHD is colorless, or maybe black, or maybe green. Yeah, green. ADHD looks like toxic green paint dripping all over the spokes of my soul. ADHD is several blackouts midsentence.

ADHD is generations of squirrels on separate wheels, running around at all hours of the day and night.

Sometimes I have several thoughts before I brush my teeth in the morning. Or maybe they are just fragments and I am kidding myself by calling them thoughts.

ADHD makes the sounds snow makes—it is silent—but the more it accumulates through the day, the heavier it gets.

CHAPTER THREE

OFF THE ROCKER

Occurred: 1996-1998

O ne fall afternoon during kindergarten I had discovered what it meant to kiss a girl from overhearing my brothers talk about it.

Around that time, I always ate lunch with a girl named Lily. She had adorable brown hair and blue eyes. She was a perfect match for me and we both knew it. She sat at the table with all my guy friends and me at lunch. In some abstracted way we were boyfriend-girlfriend, or at least we claimed to be, and we wrote cute letters to one another in class.

She was always two people in front of me in line because her last name was Robinson, right behind her was Paula Anderson, and then Smith (me). I swear Meredith hated me because I forever smiled past her at Lily—she would kick me and shove me. Man, I was scared of Paula.

But back at the lunch table, Lily, my male cohorts, and I, sat in a circle. To my right I passed on a secret to my friend Paul. "Lily should kiss Andrew, pass it on," I whispered. Paul laughed and passed it on.

As time expired during lunch the cat came out of the bag. Lily had heard the news and she whispered in my ear. "During last recess, I will be waiting for you by the gym." My heart fluttered, and I felt trepidation in my bones. I didn't even know what trepidation was, but I was about to experience Lily's wet red lips on mine.

The clock ticked and the bell rang, recess was now in session, and everyone scrambled from their desks toward the playground. It was like a mirage: all the students in the class moved at full speed while Lily and I moved in slow motion, two small blobs drifting toward the location. My friend Harry came with me and Lily brought a friend with her. Harry stood behind me, while Lily's friend stood behind her and kept watch for administration.

Lily stood patient as a turtle and looked directly into my eyes. I reciprocated; our eyes locked. I stepped closer, and her face became bigger. We were at a threshold, and then we closed our eyes as our lips agreed to meet. Then all four of us giggled as we separated in sequence and ran to the playground. I was a whole new man. I was high on life. The next day in class she and I had a secret.

Time passed and I graduated kindergarten and moved across the hall to first grade. My teacher was Mrs. Payne. I remember half way through the year my friend Paul and I were doing arts and crafts and we played with the supplies. There were some cotton balls and we thought it would be fun to shove them up our noses. So we did. But one of the cotton balls got jammed in my right nostril. The more I picked at it, the higher up my nostril it traveled, and for some reason I was without worry.

My teacher was quick to notice and took me to the principal's office where I met bald Mr. Walker . I ended up having to go see a doctor later that day. He tried to pry the cotton ball out of my nose with tweezers, but it was crammed up there. I was so embarrassed about the art project gone awry. That left only one scenario: they had to knock me out with anesthesia and surgically remove the cotton blob. The next week at school, my friends thought it was marvelous, so this only pushed me higher into the popular limelight.

Then my parents switched me and my brothers to the local elementary school by our house, Westgate Elementary. I was crushed that I had to leave behind my girl Lily and wingman Harry. I arranged my valediction, and began my new life at Westgate. This was where my neighbor Olivier Mars and I became best of friends. He had five brothers and was the popular kid at Westgate. He and I walked to school together, he introduced me to the people he knew, and I began to become popular once more. And that was when I met Mika Hoff.

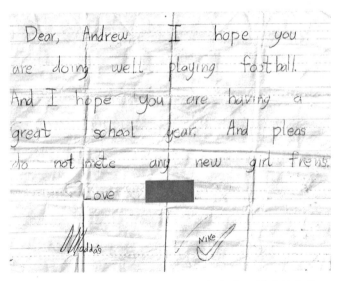

This is a letter Lily wrote to me in first grade before I left Holy Rosary.

Lets skip through second grade and move to third grade, where my hyper-activeness caught up with me and I began to make far worse mistakes. Mrs. Flowers switched around the seating arrangement part of the way through third grade, putting Olivier in a different class, so I was forced to make some new friends. The altered seating arrangement allowed me to meet the voracious girl named Mika. She sat directly next to me and we started to get along well. She had black hair and wore a black necklace snuggly around her neck. She and I developed crushes on each other.

Then one day she tapped me on the shoulder. "Want to hang out after school today?" I nodded and continued to work on my prime numbers.

I had no idea something very romping was about to occur.

After school Mika came over to my house with my neighbor Blake to hang out. They brought over a game to play that I was unfamiliar with at the time. The game was Twister, and I was a Twister virgin. Mika pulled the game out of her backpack and set it up. The game did not look anything like a vicious storm. I was intrigued.

We were downstairs with no supervision and we started to twirl the spinner. I ended up positioned spread eagle doing a backwards push up type stance with Mika beneath me. Blake was lucky and got stuck on the edge.

Things escalated and Mika and I wound up in the bathroom downstairs while Blake kept watch outside the door for parents. We

This is me in 3rd grade holding up my name card.

stood facing each other and she spoke quietly, "You can do anything you want to me." I figured it was time I moved on from Lily, and so I nervously remarked, "You start." She shook her head no. I had a bad case of the butterflies. I felt like a schoolboy. Then I wiggled my toes and proceeded toward her and kissed her, tongue and all. I am sure it was the most pathetic thing ever. We definitely tongue scraped, but we managed not to hit teeth, so that was to our advantage.

Then Blake knocked on the door and blabbed, "Almost done?" Mika and I stopped kissing and were now having a staring contest. She wanted to do more. In a soft voice, she said, "You can do anything you want to me," but I was a wimp. I pondered if I should chicken out or not.

We stood there and hopelessly gleamed deep into one another's eyeballs for a good five minutes. Crazy thoughts were going through my head. I did not know what sex was yet, so thoughts of cooties and my mom walking in was as far as my mind could go. Then a thought struck me: was it too late? Had I just been infected with cooties from Mika? I was going nutty trying to collect all my thoughts. I can only imagine what Mika was thinking. Then she walked toward the door, opened it, and it was all over.

Third grade came to a close and I graduated to fourth grade. My teacher was Mrs. Jenkins and I ended up having Olivier in my class that year, along with his cousin Riley. They kept me out of trouble for the better part of fourth grade.

Mika's home life was rough and she once acted out by attempting to commit suicide by choking herself in class. All in all, I believe I saw this wave of a blue gel penned girl scampering down the school hallways—fleeing onward, trying to escape because of her jangly homelife and dark thoughts, both of which I was into. Not that my homelife was bad, but because I felt like I was a singular soul among my cohorts. We connected like magnets and I tried to be a rebel with her because I was a psycho in my own right, though not as much of one as she was.

Her choking incident was when Olivier helped me realize that she was crazy and the crush for her diminished. I then started to have a new crush or girl, Monica, and we would talk until we were blue in the face.

Half way through fourth grade my parents took my brothers and me to Australia to visit Spencer and Paige Bo, some family friends. I missed two weeks of school because we were there for a month, just after the 2000 Summer Olympics in Sydney. The first week there we were on the beach and I saw a girl with her top off. I fell to the ground and laughed and laughed. That was the first time I had seen two scoops of matter dangling in front of my eyes. I was wigging in the sand, astounded and mesmerized, as my parents giggled at me.

I forever can't unsee that moment in time. Being exposed to that pair of boobs changed me. I saw a live rack at the age of ten, and there was no going back. Later on during the trip I got an ear infection when I swam through the fierce waves on Bronte Beach. That made me vomit and I was under the weather for most of the rest of the vacation.

Scientists have done studies about people who get ear infections when they are younger and have shown that they are more likely to become distracted and have ADHD symptoms. The vacation was a small clip into the biological changes of my body and may have played a part in the antics I would be involved in when I returned from Australia.

When I got back, I was popular because I had missed school and traveled. People thought it was cool, which was totally unintentional. I was tired of being popular. When I returned my assigned seat was next to Monica, the girl I liked, which was lucky and also unlucky.

Inside the Adderall Empire
FRAGMENT THREE

My thoughts twist and twirl into a new space. The life of a person with ADHD is an unconnected, discombobulated, scrambled passion for life. Constantly distracted from the norm, I hang around the equator of life, bouncing back and forth on an infinitely thin line.

I only manage to keep on that track for brief segments of time, when fresh new experiences cloud my brain and keep me fluttering up and down near the equator—lost and confused—barely connected to the mundane essentials of the world.

I wanderlust through different people's viewpoints, fading in out like a camera lens. My thoughts travel through the souls of new friends and old, through technology and in person, joking and teasing, laughing and being serious, doing figure eights, getting lost on the path. Now I am doing figure eighty-eights, banging through the minds of the new and unordinary.

Bursting to help, to be helped. But here I go: strapping down into the ADHD cannon and shooting off into the world.

I move. I am too hot to handle the eccentricities of this life.

Being ADHD is a job, a job that is forever. I cant un-be ADHD. But it is not only being ADHD; it is more than that. It is the fresh new thoughts that bloom in my brain, creating a mirage that touches different ecotones.

CHAPTER FOUR

SCHOOL ANTICS
Occurred: 1999 to 2005

A fter I graduated fourth grade I applied to be on cross-guard duty. It was something my brother had done and he had been one of the captains, so I wanted to follow in his footsteps. When fifth grade rolled around I was all trained and was supposed to be a leader because I would go to school early and wear the white helmet, carry a flag to the crosswalk, and help my cohorts cross the street. Life was good and I was happy—at least I thought I was—but I began to act up in fifth grade for no reason at all.

A few weeks into school, Dentyne Ice reached the market and my parents always made sure I had money on me, so I purchased the minty gum. My teacher was not a fan of gum in her class; I had Mrs. Jenkins once more, and she caught me one day chewing the sticky refreshment. So I spat it out but mischievously put another piece in my mouth when she turned

This is me on June 18th, 2001, in my cross guard uniform before I got kicked off the squad.

to face the chalkboard, because she had not taken the pack from me. When she caught me again, my classmates laughed, and she took me to the principal's office. Lame, I thought.

They said I was not setting a good example for the rest of my classmates, and kicked me of cross-guard duty. They thought if they kicked me off cross-guard duty it would show my classmates that it was bad to chew gum, and they used me to teach the rest a lesson. But did they really believe that I was going to just not be a leader anymore?

Soon thereafter I discovered what "gay" means. I had gotten the impression that my fourth grade band teacher, Mr. Port, was gay because he was always wearing tight shirts and talking about his male partners in some way. During band practice, I played my trumpet and tried to get stars for playing songs correctly, but I was constantly distracted.

I rebelled. One day in class, when he wasn't looking, I graffitied "Mr. Port is gay" on a music stand. After I wrote it a few times, he noticed and addressed the class, asking who had done it. My band mates peeped their eyes in my direction so I raised my hand and admitted that I had done it.

"Andrew! I want to see you outside."

So I followed him outside and we sat down at a desk in the hallway. He grabbed my arm. "What's wrong with you? Huh? My beliefs are my business, and they're between me and the guy upstairs."

My shoulders were slouched as I tried not to look him in the eyes. "Sorry," I sputtered in a low voice.

"No. I don't think that you are sorry," he said, eyes glaring into mine. "You are not allowed in band anymore." He stood up and dragged me around the corner to my teacher's room. Mrs. Jenkins was sitting at her desk with a bunch of papers and appeared to be doing something important.

He burst into the room, toting me by the arm, and furiously announced, "He is out of band permanently!" He huffed out of the room to teach the rest of band practice. I stood there, still slouched. Mrs. Jenkins looked up, a little bewildered, and didn't seem sure of what to do with me. She put her papers down. "Come with me, Andrew," she said, and I slogged behind her to the front office where she dropped me off. I was not her problem anymore. The office was not sure what to do with me either. Eventually someone took me to the crazy kid class.

Everyone knew about the crazy kid class. Everyone knew the crazy kids got yelled at. Everyone was scared of that class. And so was I.

The principal lugged me through the hallway and explained that I had to spend the remainder of the week there. When I arrived, there were kids who were, in some ways, similar to me: wild, confused, not thinking before acting, being immature, and so on. I refused to participate in class, was silent the whole time, perhaps because I was in denial that I was like them. It felt like elementary school prison.

After the week came to a close I was mortified. The school's plan to scare the trouble out of my soul was working. At least I thought it was, and so did they.

Until a month later, when I was walking home with the kids from my school who lived in my development. We were walking down 96th street and Monica and I were rattling off words. William's house was getting close. Across the street we spotted a girl named Stacey who had just moved to our development. Monica yelled, "William and Stacey want to take sponge bath together."

I jumped right in, singing, "Yeah, Stacey loves taking sponge baths, her parents are lesbians!"

Somehow I knew the small detail, but did not know what it meant. William stayed out of the whole conversation, crossing the street to his house. Monica and I were persistent on the bubble bath concept and kept playing off each other's words.

"Stacey likes bubble baths with her rubber ducky," I yelled. It was not totally apparent to me what I was yelling to the girl, but she got annoyed and, when she reached her house, she told her parents we sexually harassed her.

The next day Monica and I were pulled into the principal's office; they were furious at us for not following the Westgate Way motto. They claimed that we were sexual harassing the poor girl and we each got one week of in-school suspension. I sat in an entryway into the main office with my lunch and schoolwork. Monica was in the librarian's office, where she stuck out her suspension. Every day, administration walked by and glared at me with their demon eyes, like *I* was the devil. Once a day for seven days my teacher dropped off the work she had assigned in class.

Those days at school were painful, and back at home my parents had put me on restriction. The trust level had been lowered once again.

It felt as if I had morphed into a bad kid when I returned to class. Everyone looked at me differently, even my friends Olivier and William. I was starting not to fit in anymore. Stories of what I'd done had spread and had pushed me past a threshold, like I wasn't a nice person anymore, like I'd become debauched.

But Monica and I had not learned our lesson. We were two sexual kids.

A month had passed since the incident and it felt like things were returning to normal. I had gained the trust back from my parents and the trust of the school was pending.

But then, for some odd reason, Monica and I made a bet over which was bigger: her boob size or my dong size. So we cooked up this competition— she would measure her boobs and I would measure my dong, and we'd compare. So during class I pulled out a piece of paper and a pen and took the bathroom pass to the bathroom.

I got hard and slapped my penis down on the piece of paper and marked the piece of paper where the tip of my penis hit from the end of the page. I zipped up my jeans and walked back into the classroom, slipping her the piece of paper. She got up to use the bathroom next, and came back with a mark on the paper. It didn't make much sense, and wasn't a very accurate way to compare such things, but we were curious and our classmates were starting to get excited about the results.

As soon as the recess bell rang, Monica, our friend Tiger , and I ran out to the woodchips to see the results of our investigation. Tiger was new to our class, and we'd adopted him into our bad-kids group. I don't think he'd quite processed the bad kid part yet.

Somebody had eavesdropped on our snickering during class and had tattled on us to Kutcher, the recess supervisor. I looked up from the sheet in my hands to see her marching toward us from across the kickball field, pumping her arms and frowning angrily. She blew her whistle and yelled, "Andrew! Give me that piece of paper!" Just before she approached us, we dug a hole in the woodchips and buried the sheet. But she'd seen us do it and saw the guilt that glowed on our faces as she bent down and brushed away our lame attempt at hiding the evidence.

She saw the marks on the paper and confirmed that we had been measuring our private parts. What otherwise would have appeared as a piece of paper with pen marks on it made her face crunch up. She was "appalled at our behavior," and she made Monica and me stand on the wall the rest of recess to "think about what you have done." I guess she knew Tiger was new and let him go, but I caught a snippet of her scolding him for not thinking twice about hanging around with troublemakers.

When the bell rang signaling the end of recess, Kutcher took us to the main office and reported our antics. The ladies in the office were instantly mad at us. They were fed up with our games and they all started weighing in on how to punish us—even the ones who didn't usually work in the office. They decided that more in-school suspension was in order. So back to our spots we went for silence and seclusion from class.

That first day while I was back at the desk in the hallway, I heard the principal making calls to Monica's parents and mine. She wanted to meet with my dad to tell him what had been going on, explain my "overly sexual behavior" at school, and somehow try to "fix" me.

I sat there until the end of the day. When my dad came to pick me up, he walked right past my desk to enter the principal's office with a sigh. He seemed stressed out. I stayed at the desk, an earshot away from my father and the principal.

"I am Andrew's dad. Here to pick him up," he said to her.

The principal said, "Hello Mr. Smith. Ah…Does your son masturbate often?"

My dad sounded disgusted. "I don't know," he said. "What kind of question is that?"

"Monica and Andrew measured their private parts today. The office staff and I think you should a conversation with him about it. I also think it's a good idea that Monica and Andrew don't see or talk to each other anymore."

I heard them get up and push in their chairs. I pointed my head forward so it didn't look like I'd been listening the whole time, then sat, bug eyed, looking guilty and worried. They walked over to me and my dad dragged me to the car. I saw the disappointment in his eyes as he drove me home. The trust was gone again. My parents did not know what to do with me.

When we got home, my dad sent me to my room. My mom came home and I imagine he told her what had happened. They called me down to explain my punishment: I was supposed to clean up our dog Sonic's poop in the backyard for a week. I refused to do it and I yelled at my dad, who proceeded to try to spank me. They had always spanked me when I did something wrong, but I was old enough then to have heard that spanking was not allowed. "Stop it or I will tell the cops on you!" I screamed.

I tried to wrestle him—father and son, battling it out. Finally, we let go of each other and I lay on the floor. I was mad, he was mad.

"Fine!" he bellowed. "I won't spank you anymore." He panted and caught his breath. "But damnit, I don't know what else to do!"

"I am not doing anything you say!" I growled.

"If you're not going to listen to me, then I am going to take you to the police. And *they* can deal with you!"

He yanked me by the neck of my shirt and told me to get into the car. He got in and slammed the door, starting the engine and jerking the wheel as we backed out of the driveway.

I seethed in the back seat, too angry to consider what was about to happen as he spouted off about me being crazy and not listening to him. The words stuck to my heart like Velcro. He drove us to the Edmond's Police Station and we both slammed our butts into seats in the waiting room. He was trying to be a good dad, he said, and had no idea what to do to get me to stop. I was a loose cannon.

I looked around the police station as fear, anger, sadness, and irritation gushed through my entire body. I hated myself for the pain I could so clearly see in my father, for the pain I had brought on my family.

After a few moments I agreed to do the things he asked and he drove me back home. The trip to the police station was the moment when I knew I was messed up and needed to get my life on track.

———

The school year slugged on after that, but it was an awful time for me. I wasn't allowed to talk to Monica anymore, and everyone's parents told their kids not to hang out with me. It felt like I'd become the classroom villain. Somehow I did manage to friend a girl named Shannon. She was a beautiful blonde who dressed in Roxy clothing, and I considered us boyfriend and girlfriend because I would hug her after each recess before we headed back to class. She never fully hugged me back, though.

My best friend Olivier told me he was not supposed to spend time with me anymore and I was so sad because I felt like I had no one left—not one friend.

Even P.E. class stopped being fun. I wound up making friends with the teacher, Mr. Sones . He was a bald African-American fellow and an assistant coach for the Meadowdale high school basketball team. He and I would sit and talk during class and he'd tell me about how he played basketball at Wisconsin. He knew about the Monica scandal and would let me play my Nelly CD before the start of P.E. as we ran in circles for three minutes. He called me "Playboy" and, when everyone played the activity he had arranged for the day, we sat and talked about life.

All that changed one day when Mr. Sones was sick and I had a substitute teacher for class. My friends and I had recently discovered Eminem and Dr. Dre, so we listened to rap music—secretly, of course, because our parents would never have let us listen to CDs with 'Parental Advisory' slapped on the front cover.

Dr. Dre used this word, "nigger," in one of his songs, and I hadn't figured out exactly what that meant or if it was bad. I knew that was what black people were sometimes called, but I had no idea it was offensive. So when Mr. Sones was gone I called a kid in my class, Shawn, who was black, a nigger. I couldn't let it go and kept yelling it in his face as I ran in circles around him. "Nigger, nigger, nigger!" I yelled as I chased him.

It was not that I disliked him—we were cool and content with each other—but I was crazy. I had hurt his feelings, but he did not say anything at first.

Later that week we had P.E. again and the girls in my class told Mr. Sones about what I had done. The girls were crowded in his office, comforting Shawn, and Mr. Sones spoke with him for a while as well. Then Mr. Sones called the principal. She came over and, once she heard what I had done, she grabbed me and told me I was on in-school suspension again for another week. She made me apologize to Shawn's and his mother.

I felt awful. I was not racist at all. I was just a stupid little kid who started using a word before learning its meaning. I just thought that's what cool guys called black people.

My mom was furious with me. I could tell she was mortified. She said the principal had called to question her about if she and my dad were racist. Of course she denied it—my parents had close friendships with black people and loved black people the same as white people. This event made me realize that the school was starting to judge my parents because of my actions.

I was so mad at myself. My mom made me stay in my room all day; I sat there listening to the rain pelt the side of my window. I was confused and angry. I punched my bed, furious with myself for the mistake I had made.

After the in-school suspension I returned to class. Shannon had started dating Shawn, and everyone kind of shunned me. I was a complete outcast. Everyone looked at me differently. I was spiraling. I felt like the devil. I was the devil.

I had not yet been diagnosed with ADHD, but I look back on those days and swear that's what it must have been. I was not a bad kid at heart—my intentions were good, but they had not diagnosed me yet. Instead, the school branded "troublemaker" across my chest, and I was seen as an immoral child.

Finally, fifth grade came to an end.

———————

My friend Olivier moved away that summer, too. I remember seeing the 'For Sale By Owner' sign outside of his house and feeling my stomach drop, leaving an empty, lonely ache. His house sold by the start of sixth grade and I had to say goodbye. He still accepted me as his friend, but his parents strictly forbade him from seeing me. We both knew we were going to miss each other, but there was nothing either of us could do, and when he went off to Arlington, that was that.

I was starting to make friends with Bruce Helms, Bud Tyler, and some skateboarding guys, but it was still a lonely summer.

When sixth grade started, I thought, "Sweet, a fresh start!" I'd spent the summer trying to make it up to my parents for all the stress I caused them, and

had gained some of their trust back, sprinkled with some from the administration. Other kids were talking to me more, and I felt like a more rounded human. Things were getting better.

My sixth grade teacher was Mrs. Banks and she was brand new to the school. I think my subconscious had connected the dots and taken her to be vulnerable, so we clashed from day one. I acted in the most immature ways in her classroom. I couldn't even help it—I had already established myself as the comedian of the school and was always trying to act funny. I was always talking back to her, I never tried in class, and was constantly off task.

One thing I did was break pencils on my head. This somehow became quite popular. I took a pencil and smashed it on my forehead and it snapped in half, then other classmates started doing it, and eventually kids were doing it in other classes as well. We were told that we had to stop or we would be in big trouble.

I also entertained the class by sagging my pants (Eminem and Dr. Dre had influenced me in more ways than one). It was becoming a popular thing and other kids mimicked my ways, so then one day Mrs. Banks decided to make an example of me. She stopped the entire class and raised her voice. "Pull up your pants, Andrew."

My boxers were sticking out but I tried to pull them up. "There you go."

She yelled louder, "Farther Andrew. I can see your boxers."

I was starting to get mad. "I can't pull them up any farther!"

"Andrew, come on. Farther!" Everyone was beginning to laugh at me instead of with me, and it made me even more mad. Later that day she called my mom and said that she wanted to have a parent-teacher conference. I feared that the trust I'd slowly gained over the summer was going to slip away, but I denied that anything was wrong when my mom mentioned the call. Mrs. Banks hadn't gone into specifics. The day of the conference came and she told my parents about the sagging pants incident. She told them I was making it difficult for her to create an environment for kids to learn, and that I didn't take standardized tests seriously. That did not sit well with my mother, and it was basically unspoken that I'd be put on restriction again. The trust was slipping through my fingers; I felt so ashamed of myself. Luckily no one in class knew about the conference. My friends still accepted me, but that was my only bead of positive news.

The rest of that school year was simply endured. I didn't realize it at the time, but since the administrators thought so little of me and I refused to get along with Mrs. Banks , I was harboring a lot of resentment toward the school. My skateboarding buddy Bud had his beef too, so we started creating pranks to get back at them.

For example, during our last three months at Westgate we peed on the water heaters in the bathroom. It was Bud's idea at first but by that time I had trouble saying no to anything that would make things harder for the school. Soon after, though, the teachers started to hear complaints from the janitor, who did not want to clean up the puddles we were leaving in the bathroom. The teachers held a meeting for the sixth grade, asking if anyone knew who was responsible. They told everyone that the person should turn themselves in.

Bud and I had no intentions of turning ourselves in, but we had told a few friends what we were doing. The gossip trickled down into the ears of one of the teachers and I was pointed out as the main suspect. They sat me down to interrogate me, and I was such a terrible liar that I just fessed up, but Bud didn't. Nobody told on him and he never came forward. So they found a punishment perfect for the crime. The principal personally delivered me to the janitor, who handed me a mop and a bucket. I was ordered to clean all the bathrooms in the school for two days.

It was awful. Every swing of the mop was full of rage. Plus, I went home both days smelling like cleaner. How come I was the only one to get in trouble? It was not even my idea to begin with! But I had done it, so I deserved to play janitor. Stinky, sweaty janitor. My parents' trust in me sank even lower, but I was still quite popular in the class.

Graduation was approaching and Bud and I had one last prank to pull before we graduated. Rather than teaching me a lesson or dissuading me from acting out, the water heater incident had filled me with hunger for payback. Both mine and Bud's older brothers had showed us how to TP and egg a house, and one day when his parents were gone and his brothers were babysitting, he called me to come over. Bud was smart and told his brothers we were going to walk his dog. Instead, we scored the spare toilet paper from his garage, six eggs from his fridge, and placed all the supplies in backpacks and walked to the school. It was around eight o'clock at night. We told each other, "Let's get in and get out. No hanging around on this one—no getting caught." So we tied his dog to the playground bars, split up the supplies, and did our magic. We grabbed the dog and sprinted back to his house safely without raising any alarm.

The next day, there was a meeting in the entryway with all the students. They told us the janitor had witnessed kids doing it, that they found dog hair, and that they were going to prosecute the culprits. Bud and I kept our mouths shut, too nervous to even exchange glances.

They never caught us, but that was probably the last time I did something wrong without getting caught. Looking back, I see that I was troubled, but my morals were not necessarily bad.

Sixth grade graduation didn't come a day too soon. The summer went by and I spent most of my time skateboarding with Bud.

———————

Seventh grade was a whole new animal: College Place Middle School. I made a couple new friends and my best friend was a girl named Mackenzie. I started to take a bigger interest in girls once middle school started and I dated a few of Mackenzie's friends. I was pretty normal for the start of seventh grade.

I didn't smoke weed in seventh grade—this would come later. But because I was friends with all the stoners, and because I would go crazy and disturb class by throwing things and talking when I wasn't supposed to, people got the impression that I was a stoner, too. This behavior caused me to get sent to an area at College Place Middle called 'Time Out.' I was sent there a lot. It resembled the crazy kid classroom I had encountered at Westgate. Except this one usually had one to three people in it at a time. The lady who ran Time Out was scary and would yell at us all the time.

Eventually eighth grade rolled around and I was fourteen years old, nearing fifteen by the end of the school year. People at school saw me as the wild one, always running around laughing and doing crazy things. I was dating a lot of girls, too. I was known for having made out with about five different girls. This made me popular, but I started to get myself into more and more trouble. Popularity was my kryptonite. The more popular I got, the more recklessly I acted.

One girl I dated, Vanessa, belonged to the group of kids who smoked weed. I also had friends from elementary school who were starting to do that kind of stuff. We dated for a month or so but she ended up breaking up with me. I was crushed, so I started hanging out with my friends William and George Mazzerati. They tried drinking and smoking before me and I was intrigued, but was still against the notion.

Second trimester rolled around and I was in class with my friend Hugh when I got the idea to stash gum in my math teacher's coffee. Morris was always rude to me because I wasn't any good at math. And probably because I didn't pay attention. I thought I would get back at her, so Hugh helped me come up with a prank. At the beginning of class she had her coffee like usual, and when she dipped off to the bathroom before class started we spotted it next to the projector. Once she left I nonchalantly walked up to the projector, spat my gum into my hand, and dropped it into the cup. It plinked and sank, invisible at the bottom of the cup. Class went on and Hugh and I snickered every time she sipped her coffee. We started to worry that she was getting suspicious, but she couldn't pinpoint what we were up to. Finally the class finished and we escaped, saluting one another and going our separate ways to second period.

After we left, some kid in the class approached her and tattled on me. She must have marched over to the principal's office and told him what I had done. Mackenzie worked for the office as a messenger that delivered slips to classrooms, so when the principal wrote a slip and gave it to her to deliver, she found me in my English class and gave the teacher the slip. I exited class, and she was waiting there to tell me that I was screwed and Waibler was enraged. Then she scurried to the office before me so it didn't look like I knew her. She thought it was funny, and so did the friends I told in my next class.

But, in that moment, thoughts bounced like crazy off the walls of my skull, and I was terrified. I decided that I was going to deny it and say that whoever told on me was lying.

Moments later I arrived at the office and walked past Mackenzie. We didn't say a word to each other as I walked to the front desk and flashed my slip. The secretary took my slip and muttered, "So you're the guy. Well, come with me." We walked into the principal's office and Morris was still in there to welcome me with the meanest, most disgusted look ever.

I said, "What? Why am I here?"

Morris stomped off, giving me the stink eye. Then the principal told me to sit down and began his interrogation. He held a mug up to my face. "How did this gum get here?"

I rolled my eyes. "I don't know what you're talking about."

He set the cup on the table, leaned forward, and looked me dead in the eyes. I was terrified, trying to keep my composure. "I know you did it," he said in a stern voice.

I sat and said nothing, and I was doing good until he said, "If you fess up now I will give you two days suspension. If not, you're getting five days."

Dammit, I thought to myself, *I don't want five days*. I hated that he had broken me down. "Fine," I sneered at him.

"So you did do it? I knew it!" and he slammed his palm on his desk.

I was so mad. He tricked me, but really it was my fault. I had done it, so I deserved whatever was coming. The principal followed through with the punishment and suspended me for two days. But he also told my football coach and made me write a letter of apology to Morris. That sucked.

This was the kind of trouble that I always seemed to be in. I felt like I was stuck in a vicious cycle of trying to make my friends laugh, then getting in heaps of trouble for it.

And of course my mother and father were furious at me again. They told me they loved me no matter what, but gosh were they mad. They had no more trust in me. I was back to the task of gaining that back, all because of a stupid piece of gum. The restriction my mom put me on me sucked, but my football coach finding out was far worse. When I returned to school after missing two days of practice, he stopped everyone at practice and made me do up-downs from one end zone to the other in front of the entire team. Every time he blew on the whistle, I would drop to the ground and I could hear my entire football team laughing at me. I was beyond embarrassed. I wanted to sprint away and never come back.

During these days, I thought about running away a lot. I thought that if I ran away my parents would finally be unburdened. They would no longer have to deal with me. I would be doing them a favor. One day while I was on restriction I told my mom I was going to run away. I sprinted out of the house, around the corner, and found a bush to sit in. I shoved my face in my palms, racked with anger and sadness that seemed to blend together. Eventually I stood up and decided I would walk down to my grandma's place; she lived just ten minutes from my house.

As I walked, I stewed, ashamed of myself. I did not want to live in my life anymore. I kept screwing up and didn't see a way out of all the turmoil I'd created. I was approaching rock bottom. I say that in retrospect, knowing now what rock bottom really feels like. But at the time, I felt as if I were at the top of a waterfall, falling forever with no splash. Just the ache of that threshold, the anger at the world. I saw no solution.

My grandma called my mom when I arrived. She came to pick me up, took me home, and I was sent straight to my room. No dinner for me tonight, I thought. I don't deserve it.

At school there was good news and bad news. The good news was, everyone thought I was funny for the prank I pulled on Morris. And that made up for things a little. But the bad news was that I was stuck with Morris. There was tension between us for the rest of the year. I knew she hated me and she knew I dismissed her. I couldn't get myself to learn any math in her class. Her patience with me was nonexistent. This is part of the reason I am bad at math to this day.

In the final few months of the semester, I had my first experiences with cigarettes, weed, and alcohol. But my grades turned out to be some of my best, so I adopted a notion that I'd be able to multitask between substances and school.

The first time I drank was with my friend Bon. I filled two Propel bottles halfway with gin and topped them off with orange Juice. I brought the bottles to school with me and handed one to Bon, keeping the other for myself. We drank all through Morris's class. We were stuck in the corner because she did not pay much attention to us, only to the ones she thought had futures. So we sat and gulped the bottles down, making funny faces the whole time.

By the end of the class, I was drunk. And so was he. It felt unreal and I walked to my next class feeling like a superstar, talking it up with my friends like I usually do. It was amazing. Then it wore off halfway through gym class. That day, I also experienced my first hangover.

I enjoyed the feeling though, and I thought it might be good for me. I felt like it allowed me to extinguish the perfectionist tendencies I had started to develop. More importantly, it allowed me to forget about the people I had let down, especially my parents.

This was when I became closer with William, Mazzerati, and Brandon, who we called Sandman. We would all meet at my neighbor Max's house at the end of Spruce Street and drink in his basement. Sandman was ahead of his time and was able to get us forties of beer. Our drinking routine started there in "the Dungeon."

Eighth grade was coming to a close, and my grandpa knew I was going to get my permit when I turned fifteen, so he took me out to a parking lot one day and let me drive. He showed me how the parking brake worked, how to turn on the lights, and how the car would drift forward when you put it in drive. I thought I was an expert driver that day. So, naturally, I wanted to show my friends.

My parents were at one of my brother's baseball games and I told them I would be at a friend's house, but we all went over to my house. William and George ate goldfish and drank Gatorade in my yard, having a good old time. Then I told them I knew how to drive and looked at my mom's black Honda Accord that was sparkling in the driveway. They were intrigued and continued to eat goldfish in my driveway while I went upstairs and found the key. I hurried back downstairs to get into the car. They all giggled as I started up the engine. I adjusted the seat so that I could see. I was pretty tall for my age, about five-foot-six, so seeing was a non-issue. I had forgotten to take the parking brake off though, and I placed the car in reverse and backed slowly out the driveway. There was an oncoming car a mere fifty feet from me as I turned toward the open road. I looked over my left shoulder as I passed an old lady and her granddaughter. She pointed at me. How could she know, I thought, quickly speeding up, clunking along.

Then I saw in my rearview mirror that the lady had pulled into my driveway and was yelling at my friends. My friends made a break for it between some houses and my heart started to race. I crept forward on the road and saw that she was behind me now, honking. I punched the gas pedal and started speeding more, but it was hard to accelerate because the parking brake was still on. I was in too much of a panic to notice though, and took a right onto the main road, 96th Street, then quickly took another right onto a side street. I was a so nervous that I forgot to use my signal.

Halfway down that side road I saw her still chasing after me and I turned sharp to my left around the corner. She was right on my ass this time and a stop sign was ahead of me. I ran it—I was so scared. I saw another side road to my left that connected back onto 96th so I took a left there, and at this point stinky smoke started steaming out of my back tires, but I didn't connect the dots. I kept going and sped down the side road till I hit 96th and ran the stop sign, then slammed the gas even harder. But the car was refusing me and the lady was persistent. Finally I managed to get the car moving fast enough to get a decent lead and I bee-lined for my house.

I took a sharp left, almost crashing into my own street sign, and pulled into the driveway to see that my friends had returned to their posts. Eating goldfish. Drinking Gatorade.

I put the car in park, turned it off, opened the door, and was hit with the smell of smoke billowing from beneath the tires. My friends were yelling, "You're the man!" But we had no time to celebrate before we saw the old lady cruising down my street. At once, I yelled, "Runnnnnnn!" All of my friends took off and I ran inside, closed the garage door, sprinted upstairs, and peeked through the blinds. The lady was parked in my driveway with her cell phone in her hand. Then she got back in her car and drove off. I waited there, my heart thumping inside my chest, the smoke evaporating in the wind.

Then a cop pulled into my driveway. He got out, looked around, came up my front steps, and knocked on my front door. I chose not to answer so he walked down the steps, got back into his car, and left. My friends slowly came creeping back to my driveway and I opened up the garage. We laughed and talked about how awesome that just was.

I couldn't believe I had gotten away with it. Somehow I was lucky enough on that one to not get into trouble. But still, a realization was starting to creep into my guilty head that I was out of control, and it scared me. I had to rationalize it: my friends wouldn't think what I was doing was so funny if it wasn't ok, right? But the rationalizations never really worked. I was becoming more and more worried about surviving in society, and I started to drink more.

———

The last day of eighth grade was only days away, but I got into a tussle. It was P.E. and I was sitting out in the grass when I saw a kid I recognized from Time Out, one of the crazy kids. He came up to me looked me straight in the eyes, then threw a rock at me. He gave me this nasty smirk and said, "What you going to do about it?"

I knew he thought I would be too shocked, that I would blow it off, but I called his bluff. I sprang up and shouted "Fuck you!" His face got red—he hadn't expected that, and he shoved me. That infuriated me, so I clenched my fist and swung at him, grazing the top of his forehead. He backed off and put his hands in the air. Mine were in the air as well, and the kids in P.E. started to surround us. Then he swung at me, scraping my ear, and the crowd cheered us on.

I spat in his face, which made him even angrier, and he swung at me again. I dodged the punch and made a right hook back at him. I eased up at the last second, hardly pressing against his cheek. Then Mr. Perry, the P.E. teacher, busted in, broke us up, and sent us to the principal's office.

Since he pushed me first I had an argument that he started it. And that's what I went with when I told my side of the story. He manned up and admitted that he'd pushed me first. The principal said he couldn't punish me for something I didn't start, and the kid I fought was going to Disney Land the next day, so he didn't get punished either.

This is a picture of me in 8th grade!

We both got off the hook. That's how I ended the school year. I went out with a bang and started wondering whether I was a violent person at heart, whether I was wild, or whether I was just distracted.

PART II

DIAGNOSIS

Official Medical Record

April 23, 2007
Swedish Edmonds Birth and Family Clinic
21911 76ᵗʰ Ave. W., Suite 110, Edmonds, WA 98026

Andrew K Smith
Male DOB: 06/06/1990
Patient Profile: 16 Year Male
Height: 66.75 inches
Weight: 134 pounds
Pulse rate: 88/minute
Resp: 16 per minute
BP sitting: 128/76

History of Present Illness:
Suspects has ADD, past 2 yrs…Struggles since he started high school. GPA 2.6…Trouble paying attention in class…not depressed. Feels anxious, mind races. Sometimes trouble sleeping, talks to himself and gets back to sleep… some impulsive behavior. Gets remorseful after he does something that he knows he shouldn't. Sometimes reckless driving…Suspended 2 days last yr for streaking at football game. Was not under influence…Infrequently drinks alcohol, no drugs, no tobacco.

Impressions & Recommendations:
I am uncertain of diagnosis for Andrew…Recommend that we pursue further testing.

Official Medical Record

May 15, 2007

Swedish Edmonds Birth and Family Clinic

21911 76th Ave. W., Suite 110, Edmonds, WA 98026

Andrew K Smith

Male DOB: 06/06/1990

Patient Profile: 16 Year Male

Height: 66.75 inches

Weight: 137 pounds

Pulse rate: 100/minute

Resp: 18 per minute

BP sitting: 124/82 (right arm)

History of Present Illness:

Here because his mom thinks he's depressed this past week. He is not sure. Reports that he isn't always happy. Is happy when he is around his friends… Trouble sleeping for past 1-2 years…Enjoys working out, baseball…Drugs: none…Drinks once/month, usually 3 on occasion…Plans ADD testing… He believes that his parents do not want him tested as it will "label" him.

Impressions and Recommendations:

Need for ongoing support, counseling as needed…No self-harm ideation…I also believe that his probable ADD is contributing to his underlying anxiety and frustration, and urged him to move promptly to get this tested.

Official Medical Record

September 6, 2007

Swedish Edmonds Birth and Family Clinic

21911 76th Ave. W., Suite 110, Edmonds, WA 98026

Andrew K Smith

Male DOB: 06/06/1990

Patient Profile: 17 Year Male

Height: 66.75 inches

Weight: 140 pounds

Pulse rate: 76/minute

Resp: 16 per minute

BP sitting: 122/66 (right arm)

History of Present Illness:

Was seen by Dr. Sanford who made diagnosis of ADD...Refer to previous visits here on 4/23 and 5/15.

Impressions and Recommendations:

Discuss treatment options including stimulants with discussion of common side effects, short-acting vs. long-acting options, need to titrate...He would like a long acting stimulant. Will start with Adderall.

CHAPTER FIVE

ATTENTION DEFICIENT HYPERACTIVITY DISORDER DIAGNOSIS

Occurred: Autumn 2007

I had my first appointment with the doctor, and nothing about it seemed normal to me. Her office was small, like a prison cell; the walls were blank and two-year-old magazines full of dust sat in a magazine cabinet. I sat on the loud crunchy paper and wiggled impatiently for her to arrive.

After several days at a learning center doing flash cards, answering questions, and clicking a green dot on a screen, it was official. I had ADHD. And it was in this dull cellar office that I would receive my new medication.

My doctor walked in wearing a flowered blouse and holding a clipboard with a half-concerned grimace that soured her face. I clamped my hands harder and tore small rips into the crusty paper. I've always despised the barber-esque stations I had to sit at before the doctor arrived with my future.

"How are you?" she asked, sitting down with a pen in one hand and the other hand softly pointing at me.

"I'm doing okay, hanging in there. I'm happy I'm going to get some help."

"Good Andrew, I wanted to discuss treatment options with you."

I interjected, "Medicine?"

"Yes, I wanted to discuss options such as stimulants and the side effects of long acting versus short acting medications."

"Yeah." I was worried that a medication might change me but I felt a sense of relief as well.

"Also, I wanted to review the option of an alternative non-stimulant called Strattera and the pros and cons of that versus stimulants."

"Okay."

"I'm going to tell you the common side effects, typical delay in onset of therapeutic action, and the need to gradually increase dose. I'll provide handouts with reading material for you to look over and recommendations. Alright?"

"Sure," I said, but I was not going to read material on the drug. Come on, who actually reads the two pages of medical side effects? It's like the fine print on an Apple contract. I would need a telescope or a magnifying glass and, let's be honest, it's not plausible for a sixteen-year-old kid to spend his time reading medical fine print about a drug he's taking. In a perfect world, sure, but I just wanted to take the stupid pill and see what happened.

She scooted closer to me on her four-wheel rolling chair.

"Stimulants will be something you will feel immediately upon taking in the morning and non-stimulant will take a few weeks to get into your system."

"Okay. So which one is which?"

"Strattera is the non-stimulant and if you were to take that one you would start with 20mg and build up 10mg every week for a month. What do you think about that?"

"I'm not very good at routines." I knew I would mess up and skip a day and mess up the cycle.

"Okay, so then there is Adderall, which you will feel immediately upon swallowing. Want to try that one? There are several other ones similar to Adderall. One example is Ritalin."

I felt that I was picking my fate by choosing one of these drugs. It was completely random, but Adderall had a nice ring to it.

"I'll take Adderall," I said.

"The Adderall?"

"Yes, the Adderall."

She scooted backwards in her chair, wrote on her clipboard, then pulled a prescription pad out of her pocket and wrote down "Adderall 20 Mg Tabs (Amphetamine-dextroamphetamine) 1 q am." She tore it off like she was tearing off a check from a checkbook, except my parents were the ones who were going to have to pay for the little pill.

Official Medical Record

October 4, 2007

Swedish Edmonds Birth and Family Clinic

21911 76th Ave. W., Suite 110, Edmonds, WA 98026

Andrew K Smith

Male DOB: 06/06/1990

Patient Profile: 17 Year Male

Height: 66.75 inches

Weight: 135 pounds

Pulse rate: 80/minute

Resp: 16 per minute

BP sitting: 118/68 (right arm)

History of Present Illness:

Adderall reg release did not last long enough...Notes not tired, more outgoing, better focus and concentration. All A's right now at school... Effect seems to wear off last period at school...Seeing counselor...Is starting a short-term memory program on the computer called "Cogmed."

Impressions and Recommendations:

Will try an additional dose of Adderall at lunchtime—it is his preference to drive home for this, rather than deal with medications at school, so a note was provided for this.

Inside The Adderall Empire
FRAGMENT FOUR

ADHD follows me everywhere but sometimes I can tune it out for brief periods. Drinking releases me from it but then it snaps back like a rubber band. Adderall sedates it so it doesn't bounce back as hard, but it can never be fully kicked out. Maybe Adderall puts ADHD in a timeout.

Being inside the Adderall Empire is like being in a lighthouse across the water: I can see my house, and all my friends and family can see me there, but when they see me they don't really notice me like when I get a haircut.

At night I see the others come visit me in the blinking light and they remember everything and can go anyplace they want. All the people I know are pointing at me, glancing at me, and they think it's beautiful. But inside the Empire I occupy my lighthouse and there is a moat that leads to a gate. People are crowded outside hoping to get in because it's so bright inside.

Inside the Empire I'm more visible and consistent to the outside world.

When they break into the Empire they feel free, but when they leave it's not as visible anymore. They see the blinking, the gates, and endless possibilities inside, but they only look like visitors to me. Some get tricked into thinking that it's all dandy, but it's a lonesome place and, to me, they look fake because I feel fake while inside the Empire.

The gate is two metal doors with several bars that are spiky like arrows. The gate opens outwards but it is always shut unless someone has a pill. Then when they touch the cold gate and pull on it, it will open, but otherwise one can't enter. You enter by having a pill in your hand, stomach, or pocket.

Adderall is like jumping from space. A window opens and a robust draft blasts you down through the atmosphere. Then slowly, you plunge. You and the atmosphere become the same. Then comes the moment, four minutes later, when the restraints deploy inside you. You stop soaring and drift down to ground level. A changed person, the buzzing channels in your brain form a sequence of new thoughts. The land has escaped you. You are living on a different frequency for the next six to twelve hours, or maybe forever.

PART III

POST COGMED

Official Medical Record

November 1, 2007

Swedish Edmonds Birth and Family Clinic

21911 76th Ave. W., Suite 110, Edmonds, WA 98026

Andrew K Smith

Male DOB: 06/06/1990

Patient Profile: 17 Year Male

Height: 66.75 inches

Weight: 130 pounds

Pulse rate: 78/minute

Resp: 16 per minute

BP sitting: 106/64 (right arm)

History of Present Illness:

Doing well. Memory is better. School work going well except for math. Had cog-med 1 ½ weeks ago. Is helping a lot...Patient and parent both very pleased.

Impressions and Recommendations:

Continue present medications, continue working with cog-med program. As long as grades, behavior, social issues continue to go well, next follow-up six months.

CHAPTER SIX

COGMED

Occurred: Winter 2007

S oon after streaking the football game in a bag of skin, my wild life inside the normal world transformed into a calm one in the normal world. Adderall worked, but it attacked my inner voice and I was not a talkative person anymore.

When the Adderall hit I turned silent. It ruined many situations where I could have had way more fun if I would have talked. This happened most often in the presence of girls.

Halfway through my junior year of high school, I drove with a fling of mine named Heidi to the Sheraton Seattle Hotel. It was a winter night and we were going to gawk at the 14th annual Gingerbread village display. I was wearing an ugly Christmas sweater, which was my lame attempt to appear festive. She was all dolled up in her white top with a burnt sienna scarf that matched her cinnamon hair. She always had a colossal smile with the cutest dimples that pressed her cheeks. The whole car ride there I did not speak at all. I wanted to, but words would not form into complete sentences. We spoke only about the rain that had drenched my car. It stressed me out. I wanted to say something, but what?

A few minutes later we were at the hotel and held each other's hands as we walked slowly and gazed at the gingerbread mansions.

"Whoa, look at this one Andrew, it has a chocolate syrup fountain!" she said, and squeezed my hand tighter, hopeful that I would respond.

I scratched above my right ear and mumbled, "Fountain." Gosh, it was so embarrassing. I felt wordless as my head bubbled with blood.

Somehow she was not completely annoyed with me yet and said, "I love this one. It's so cool!"

I looked at her and smirked, saying nothing. I pushed no more words out of my cerebellum that night. She knocked on my door, even rang my doorbell, but I was not home. I was somehow different – I couldn't form words out of my thoughts.

She never called or texted me again. It was another failed romance on the old belt for me, and I was in a romance with someone else—an unwanted relationship with a psycho bitch named Adderall.

I had surrendered myself to Adderall and it was eating away at my soul. Adderall had created a false perception of who I was. It made me calm, had silenced me. It was killing me, and I wanted to leave the Adderall Empire and re-enter the normal world. That's why I turned to Cogmed, an alternate method for treating ADHD.

I ended up stumbling into the office of Kristen Harris. She was a Cogmed practitioner who worked at Family Learning Strategies in Edmonds. She had a big smile, shiny white and gray hair, and a soft voice that made me feel at home. Kristen was a counselor as well as an educational ADHD specialist. She invited me in and stood near her chair, allowing me to sit anywhere I desired.

She stuck out her right hand. "Andrew, how are you?" she said the afternoon we met.

"I'm doing alright," I grunted, sprawling out on the couch with my arms crossed and my feet kicked up.

She sat. She always grinned from ear to ear. At that time, I was frustrated with myself and, naturally, I despised her grin.

"Anything new going on you wanted to talk about? Anything at all? We have a client-counselor privilege, you know? I don't tell your mom and dad about anything we have talked about."

I folded my arms tighter and said, "Yeah. I play baseball. I'm a pitcher."

Her eyes brightened up that I'd actually said something. "Wow, that's so neat Andrew. Do you like playing baseball?"

I nodded. "Yeah it's fun. It passes the time I guess."

She scooted closer to me. Things were going as planned. I was dipping into the platitudes like I always tended to do. But then she mentioned a cognitive gym called Cogmed Working Memory Training. My ears wiggled and my eyes lit up bigger than the Empire State Building on Christmas Eve.

"What's Cogmed?" I asked. My voice was starting to flutter with excitement.

"It's an experimental computer program that helps people with ADHD, invented by Dr. Torkel Klingberg in Sweden in 2001," she said.

I thought that was pretty cool, but I was skeptical. Hell, I was skeptical of everything. I was the epitome of the word skeptical.

She explained to me that it was an online computer-generated program that exercised the brain muscles. My skepticism was moving toward a cynicism vibe now, but that was just my brain fumbling. My brain thought it was too cool for the experimental journey. After an argument with my brain, I mustered up the courage and accepted the opportunity from Kristen, who was so kindly trying to help my little soul. I was about to enter what I called the "Cogmed Clubhouse."

Inside the Cogmed Clubhouse I trained on a computer program for forty-five minutes a day, repetitively performing working memory tasks—always with new and different combinations of flashing structures. As soon as I improved, the difficulty levels raised. I was pushing the limits on how much information I could remember. Working memory boosted the regions of my brain that activate and help penetrate mental functions.

I gained incredible awareness of many physiological functions by using Cogmed. Eventually I started to pick up books that had been piling up and reading them, something I have never done before. For the first time, books were thrown through the gates into my Adderall world. With the help of Cogmed, I was able to read the books and understand them.

The affects of Cogmed sometimes didn't show up until weeks after a session, but when they did show up it was a minor miracle. While on Cogmed I felt the most profound, concentrated, and noble occurrences of my life. It made me feel like my thoughts were dancing down the street like Michael Jackson on stage. I skipped on after real thoughts that interested me—the clear ones, the headache-less ones, the ones that never failed to come to mind, the fully-completed ones. The ones that never disappointed or said something inappropriate. In fact, it felt like my neurons floated out of an invisible room in my mind and through my soul, bare to the elements, and soared, soared, soared, like a meteor in the night sky. Every thought began to feel like a home run over the centerfield fence.

Where Adderall had glazed my eyes like a donut, Cogmed unglazed them. Some mornings I woke up and my eyes felt sharp and everything I thought was crisp. I could be me again but stronger, and Cogmed had been the only thing that allowed me to be Adderall-free in the normal world.

When I developed better working memory, I was happier. The doctors did a good job helping me with that, but at the same time the effects of Cogmed never fully stuck. So I would turn to Adderall for a working memory fix.

That was not the real problem though. Maybe the real problem was the shame I felt after the shinny pill was consumed. In the Adderall Empire I sometimes encountered other students as I walked along the sidewalk. We mixed our bodies with amphetamines and dove into this fake world, wandering through the streets together. Sooner or later the buildings we built together on Adderall were going to collapse like sandcastles on the beach. The college users I met came and went like strangers, but I was a permanent resident taking the stairs to the top of a lighthouse to my room, fueled by Adderall.

I felt Adderall was bad for the world—it had done nothing but give me a fabricated confidence and a feeling that I'm not good enough to focus without it. My conversations with people gave me the feeling that my thoughts were synthetic. Like sex with a prostitute—it's not the real thing.

As for the people I saw taking it recreationally, or my encounters with casual users in high school, I still don't believe it was a good thing for any of us. It made us put off time we could be spending working on assignments, and allowed us to party more by popping an Adderall last minute to bust out a good grade. It was not only that though; we lacked the confidence to do it ourselves and used Adderall as crutch.

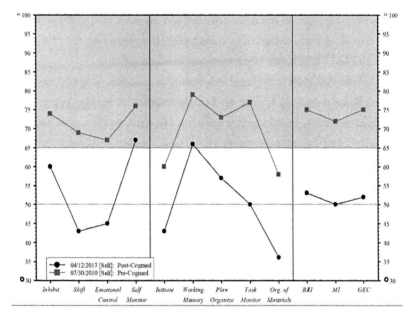

This is a graph of pre-Cogmed and post-Cogmed and how much I improved.

Sometimes I lay in bed at night and my mind was tied in a knot. Once I wondered how I touched my life-long limit of denial about needing a drug. I calculated in my head: 100,950 mg swallowed and $31,020 spent.

When Cogmed worked, when I was sober from Adderall, I had a sense of pride. It was the only time I felt freedom, felt that life was fascinating again, felt that I was the real me.

People should know who I am, not who I ought to be. But somewhere down the line I became scared to open up the doors to the real me. I was afraid of what was behind those doors. And with Adderall, I open one door and one door only: the door to the Adderall Empire.

Official Medical Record

December 13, 2007

Swedish Edmonds Birth and Family Clinic

21911 76th Ave. W., Suite 110, Edmonds, WA 98026

Andrew K Smith

Male DOB: 06/06/1990

Patient Profile: 17 Year Male

Height: 66.75 inches

Weight: 131 pounds

Pulse rate: 74/minute

Resp: 16 per minute

BP sitting: 116/74 (right arm)

History of Present Illness:

Here to follow up ADD. Decreased his afternoon dose of Adderall. Has made him tired after school so he went back up to the 20 mg dose at the advice of his counselor…Working with counselor regularly. Feels medication is doing well for him. School "pretty good." A's and B's, one C and one D, which is math…Denies feeling depressed or unhappy. Thinks medication makes him "not himself," like med is "controlling me." Feels medication is necessary to survive to be more compliant with expectations and social norm, and most of the time is worth the trade-off of not feeling like himself.

Impressions and Recommendations:

Urged him to continue counseling, and to bring up the issues of not feeling like himself with his counselor. Introduced the option of Strattera, possible benefits, differing from stimulants…ability to eliminate or reduce stimulant dose in some but not all patients. He took this information and wants to discuss with his mom before decision.

Official Medical Record

January 23, 2008
Swedish Edmonds Birth and Family Clinic
21911 76th Ave. W., Suite 110, Edmonds, WA 98026

Andrew K Smith
Male DOB: 06/06/1990
Patient Profile: 17 Year Male
Height: 66.75 inches
Weight: 132.5 pounds
Pulse rate: 72/minute
Resp: 16 per minute
BP sitting: 116/76 (right arm)

History of Present Illness:
Here to follow-up ADD. Seen alone today. Started Straterra last month. Stopped it 1 week ago because of fatigue…Did keep on regular doses of Adderall while on Strattera…Feels the same…Makes him feel shy, calmer, not "like himself." Knows it helps a lot with school performance. Seeing counselor—brought up the issue of not feeling like himself. Counselor did not offer much advice.

Impressions and Recommendations:
Discuss options…Continue Adderall as now, try a different stimulant or refer to ADD specialist. He would like to try Concerta—will discontinue Adderall and try this. Follow-up one month.

Official Medical Record

February 28, 2008

Swedish Edmonds Birth and Family Clinic

21911 76th Ave. W., Suite 110, Edmonds, WA 98026

Andrew K Smith

Male DOB: 06/06/1990

Patient Profile: 17 Year Male

Height: 66.75 inches

Weight: 139 pounds

Pulse rate: 82/minute

Resp: 16 per minute

BP sitting: 118/72 (right arm)

History of Present Illness:

Here for ADD follow-up...He is doing very well in school, excellent grades...GPA "hard to tell" but three A's and one C, in sign language. Changed from Adderall to Concerta last month, thinks he liked Adderall better. Harder to sleep on Concerta, focus not as good.

Impressions and Recommendations:

Continuing to balance benefit with side effects. Will try Vyvanse. Patient feels he will know effect promptly and wishes only two-week trial before next follow up.

Official Medical Record

March 10, 2008
Swedish Edmonds Birth and Family Clinic
21911 76ᵗʰ Ave. W., Suite 110, Edmonds, WA 98026

Andrew K Smith
Male DOB: 06/06/1990
Patient Profile: 17 Year Male
Height: 66.75 inches
Weight: 138 pounds
Pulse rate: 70/minute
Resp: 18 per minute
BP sitting: 110/68 (right arm)

History of Present Illness:
Here to follow-up ADD. Has been on Vyvanse 30 mg then 50 mg past 1 ½ weeks, but also ill with pharyngitis during this time…Not sure how new medication went—did not like it very much. Felt like it lasted too long making it harder to sleep. Focus was good, pretty much same as others. Patient prefers to go back to Adderall.

Impressions and Recommendations:
Will go back to Adderall, but on days with less need for medication he will use the lower dose. Unless problems with this approach, next follow-up six months.

Inside The Adderall Empire
FRAGMENT FIVE

Being a regulated user in the Empire is like being able to focus in the way society expects. But it's not my true identity. It's a jail in the lighthouse and that's where society pushes the ones who cause trouble. When we're sedated, we won't bother people. We're parked inside the lighthouse.

But addicts run in and out of the Empire and try to fool the world around them. It works, too, but only for so long, until they get caught.

The party people have the pill in their stomachs and travel in and out of the Empire, fooling everyone around them, including themselves. When the party's over they want nothing more than to party again. But when is enough partying enough? Some party a lot outside the Empire, then take the pill to study so they can appear like they studied more than they did. For many, this works. They take the test and that's what society measures. But a week or a month down the road, how much do they remember of what they studied on Adderall?

Study time users enter the Empire because it gives them a boost to focus and get things done. But after they use it they want to go back because the studying was beautiful and they couldn't focus as clearly. But nobody should be able to focus this much; it's not real. It's fake focus in pill form.

CHAPTER SEVEN

TWO GIRLFRIENDS
Occurred: Autumn 2007

---

here was a girl named Anna. She was perfect—everything a guy could ask for. Brown hair, voluptuous curves, and incredibly innocent. I was a junior and she was a sophomore. She did not enjoy texting so we did not talk non-stop, which was nice because some girls suffocated me through text. She and I had been dating a month and I truly liked this girl a lot.

But then I got into a situation with Sophia, who was a freshman. She was so cute and my friends told me to go for it because they thought it would be funny. She was the daughter of one of the teachers at school. So she and I went to an American Sign Language play together for extra credit and, on the way home, she unbuckled and straddled me at every stop sign and we made out. I groped her two ripe melons under her shirt—she was very developed for her age. I was having a lot of fun, so we started dating. I enjoyed this but at the same time I knew that what I was doing was wrong. I contemplated stopping, but I liked the wildness of Sophia and the innocent steadiness of Anna.

Conveniently enough I had my tonsils out and had time to get to know Sophia better through texting while marinating the norm with Anna. When I returned to school I was stuck with having to hug both of them at school. So after first period I would meet with Sophia and hug and kiss her—girls like the public display of affection. Then after the next period I would smooch Anna. I had to go home at lunch and take my Adderall every day, so I avoided having to be at lunch with them. This went on for about a week until my friends told other friends and the olive branch cracked.

Her brother found out and he was furious. He told his mother. I happened to decide to take Sophia to my house one lunch so we could get frisky. We were in pursuit of my house when I got a call from Sophia's mom. When her mom got mad, she got real mad. It was like having some crazy lady maul you with words.

"Andrew, my son is upset you're dating Sophia. I don't have a real problem with it, but if you are dating another girl, too. Then what the fuck are you doing? I swear to God you better end it and not play these games, Andrew."

Sophia was looking at me in the car and did not know who it was.

"Yeah, okay I will settle everything." Then her mom went off on a rant and swore every five words and then I hung up.

"Who was that?" asked Sophia.

"Oh it was my mom. No biggie."

I was in an utter panic. I did not know what to do or how to solve this situation, so I drove in circles through my town while Sophia sat, startled and confused. She was staring me down with her panther eyes in the passenger seat and eventually I took her back to school. When I dropped her off before the lunch bell rang, I said, "We got to break up. I am sorry."

I was so sad because I loved this wild little Greek girl but knew her mom was on my case and I didn't know what else to do.

"I don't understand. Why?" she asked.

"Just go. Leave. Get on." She sadly left.

Then I parked the car and went to my next class. I tried to pretend that everything was fine when I saw Anna after school before her mother picked her up. She had no idea what had happened.

Until the next morning, when she texted me. "You Asshole."

"What are you talking about?" I texted back.

"You know exactly what I am talking about. Meet me after 3rd period."

During 3rd period I met her and tried to get her to hear me out. I even explained my theory that I had picked her because she was the one I wanted to be with. She slapped me and said that I was a jerk and she never wanted to talk to me again. I was girless, but I did deserve it.

So I went back to my next class a single man. Halfway through class my friend Kelly said that she saw a girl in the bathroom balling that looked my girlfriend. She said she was really sad. I felt even worse.

I had tried dating two girls at once for the laughter of my friends, but I had messed up. I was an idiot. I thought I could make two girls happy at once and make my friends laugh at the same time. All would be great and dandy, but that was not how the world worked and I learned my lesson that dating two girls at once was evil.

Official Medical Record

September 2, 2008

Swedish Edmonds Birth and Family Clinic

21911 76th Ave. W., Suite 110, Edmonds, WA 98026

Andrew K Smith

Male DOB: 06/06/1990

Patient Profile: 18 Year Male

Height: 66.75 inches

Weight: 134 pounds

Pulse rate: 78/minute

Resp: 16 per minute

BP sitting: 122/72 (right arm)

History of Present Illness:

Here to follow-up ADD. Took medication through summer—had job at golf club. Started senior year this morning. Thinks medication still good dose, focus is good. Side effects not problematic, sleep okay…Will apply to Washington State University and other colleges. SAT's done, will take one more time. Will continue to work around 25 hours during school year. Still seeing counselor.

Impressions and Recommendations:

Review ADD treatment options, importance of organizational skills, refill policy…Next follow-up, six months.

CHAPTER EIGHT

UNORGANIZED
Occurred: Summer 2008

---

had surrendered myself to Adderall and it was eating away at my soul. So during the last half of my junior year of High School I decided just to drink.

I caved.

And I don't mean that I would just go out on the weekends and get casually get drunk. I mean I decided to really drink. My friend Brody and I had discovered these things called Four Loko sold at the Seven Eleven. They would get us really drunk for $2.41. We would pour the Loko in a glass and chug it in less than a minute, then wait for the alcohol to hit our blood stream. Five minutes later, we were on the threshold between drunk and blackout.

I made fake ID's in High School. I was that guy. I made a sweet template and then made them for free for my friends so I would have more people to drink with. This only escalated the drinking further. I made the fake ID's and that made me popular, then I made fake parking passes and ended up getting suspended for two days my junior year of high school.

Shortly thereafter my parents found my laminating machine tucked behind the couch, not to mention the empty bottles and Loko cans covered with blankets. As my junior year was coming to an end, my parents were becoming more and more suspicious with me. I was also starting to visit the drug and alcohol counselor at the school because I was drinking about four times a week and blacking at least one of those times. This went on for the rest of my junior year and, on the last day of school of that year, 2008, my parents really started to notice something.

The evening was a calm one, the weather was warm, and the moon was shining brightly in the night sky. My friend William came over with his girlfriend Kyra and Brody came over with his fling Audrey, who brought her friend Shailene. We hung out in my downstairs room, passing around a bottle of apple Smirnoff. I had a big room all to myself because my brothers were off at college.

We all took pulls and drank Bud Light on the side. Shailene had given me a hand job the week before, and knew I was a virgin. As we got drunker, her friends told me indirectly that she was going to have sex with me. I was enthusiastic, on the upper end of thrilled.

Shailene looked like a cute little bookworm with brown short hair, brown glasses, a huge rack, and a charming little mole on the right side of her cheek. William, a dark haired fellow with a loud voice, snuck out of the room and into the closet with his girlfriend Kyra, a cute Filipino girl. Brody, a blonde-haired, baby-faced man, followed with Audrey, who had nice curves. They went in the closet room to have sex.

Then it was me and Shailene. Like clockwork, we took of our shoes and got onto my bed and started peeling off our clothes as fast as we could—almost as fast as I did when I went streaking, but not quite. Then we were completely naked and she grabbed my pajama python and stuck it in her flesh tuxedo. After a few thrusts she said, "You're not a virgin anymore." We both giggled, we were whistling with love. A few minutes later I exhausted myself on her. I was electric, so we went for another around. I lasted much longer this time and, as I was finishing up, William came in and we went outside in our briefs and smoked a cigarette to celebrate.

He was happy for me and we both looked at the moon and laughed. When we finished our savages—that was our code name was for cigs—we went back inside. All six of us were drunk and in our underwear. Then Kyra started making out with Audrey. William and I were in heaven.

We didn't know what was going on, then someone suggested we trade girls. We were optimistic to say the least. That did not end up happening, but I wanted to have sex again, so Shay and I climbed back in bed. Apparently my dad caught William, Brody, and the girls in the hallway because he burst through the door as I was inside Shailene. She disengaged from me and I was half on top of her propped up with one arm. Then I waved my other arm at my dad and yelled, "Go away dad, I am having sex!"

Then Shay and I tried to start going at it again, but I had gotten whisky dick all the sudden. My dad was getting mad outside and William told my dad, "We all have been drinking, I will get these girls out of here."

William handled the fuck out of the situation. Anyhow, the girls left and we all went to bed. The next morning, Brody was gone, so William and I decided to go celebrate at Quiznos because that was the ritual. My mom was mad at me; I could see it in her eyes. Luckily, my dad was at work, but my mom later confiscated all my alcohol, which she found behind the couch.

Things were starting to get tense between the parents and me.

And I was beginning to feel like I was hitting rock bottom from all the drinks I was consuming. Lokos, beer—the lady at Seven Eleven knew me by name.

I've never wanted to brag—that's not what I'm doing here—but the binges of being blotto, infused with Adderall, kept me alive as an organism. Adderall forced the rational thoughts that seeped out of me, yet I lost my brains in that Adderall alcohol duo. Alcohol counteracted the alcohol and

I busted into myself, but a synthetic version of myself, with drooping and soggy neurons.

The Cogmed helped me gain my brains back, allowed me to think crisply again. But when I gained the knowledge back into my bubbling brain, I poured the alcohol in. It was a constant battle, going in and out of focus because the strict structure of today's world has me distracted. Combined with slipping memory, I turned into a walking metaphor.

CHAPTER NINE

FRIDAY NIGHT FENCE RUNNING

Occurred: Autumn 2008, and many other times

T he white picket fence looked lonesome, worn-out, and brittle. One girl was driving my car and another sat in the passenger seat. Brody and I were in the backseat. We were parked outside a random house containing the palisade. The suffering fence locked eyes with me. I squeezed my fists and scrunched my body as tight as I could while the warm heat was blowing through the heater flaps against my fair skin.

The rain outside was pelting the snow-colored car and dripped never-endingly atop the paint of the car doors. I opened the passenger side door and I could feel my friend breathing on my neck as we hysterically hoisted ourselves out of the vehicle.

Then we bolted full speed at the fence and I giggled under my breath. Multiple strides later my shoes patted the wet grass and the fence was becoming brighter. My eyes were adjusting to the night sky and I could see russet blotches that splatted across the bottom half of the wooden pickets. Moments later, with all my might, I leaped toward the fence with my right shoulder. I heard crackles that sputtered and popped. My body was unbalanced and wood splintered into pieces. I landed on the other side on top of fresh cracked boards that poked my sweatshirt. I heard my friend laughing and scrambling to get up—we were in a shuffled trance. The upper half of my body stung and adrenaline filled my head. I stepped over and through, back to the other side of the fence. My friend was directly in front of me, my clothes felt violated and wet, but we were both buzzing off the fierce encounter with the fence. We hustled back inside the backseat of the engine-running car.

This was something we called "fence running," and we did this to several broken-down fences that night. Alcohol was certainly fueling our antics. The founders of this debauched game were Brad Chinn and Drew and, eventually, it became a regular weekend activity among myself and others of the class of 2009. We took creative liberties during the night hours and fence running was among those liberties!

CHAPTER TEN

FOURSOME

Occurred: Autumn 2008

Ben Johnson and Tiffani and Peyton and I were all in my bed. I unfastened Peyton's jeans while Ben unhooked Tifanni's pants. We peeled off our clothes and all four of us were naked. Both the girls were in the missionary position. My hands were on Peyton's shoulders; her soft skin made my hands tremble. I looked to my right and Ben was inside Tiffani.

I thrusted inside Peyton, but something was in her vagina. I backed up off her while Ben started to get into a rhythm. I stuck my hand in her vagina and pulled out a bloody tampon and held it up and let it dangle as I observed it.

What the fuck? I thought. Ben laughed, "Just do it man!"

That was all the assurance I needed and I flicked the bloody piece of cotton to my left. It stuck to the linoleum floor like Velcro. Then I kissed her mouth and she lay back, ostensibly tranquil. She was widespread in the legs as I entered inside the bloody cave of her thighs.

Tiffani and Ben were glazed with beads of sweat.

Then I felt the gooey juices of her vagina and started to pump. Her mouth opened, matching Tiffani's, and the moans started to reverberate through the room. All four of us were trembling in a sensitive roar, our bodies crashing against each other. The girls' boobs were flopping in front of our eyes as we continued in motion. The bed was rocking and our eyes were wider than the girls' legs.

We were fucking.

Then, after a few minutes of utter penetration, Peyton dismounted from my cock, opened the side door, and stumbled outside. She tripped on my mother's flower pot and yacked all over. As she retched, Brody appeared through the gate to give me back the keys to my car. Both Peyton and I were butt naked. I was pissed off because Peyton was sick. Brody left the scene and I dragged Peyton inside.

Ben was still smothering Tiffani. Then Peyton yacked again all over my linoleum and I started to get more angry. I grabbed her, put her over my shoulder, and dragged her down the hallway into the bathroom. Then I ran back into my room, grabbed her clothes, threw them at her, and shut the door. Then I walked back to clean up the puke and my dad just stepped down the last step into my view. I put my hands over my privates.

"What's going on down here?"

"We are just hanging out."

Ben is fucking Tiffani and she is moaning just an earshot away.

"What's that smell?"

"Oh nothing. We will quiet down."

"Alright. Be quiet." Then he walked upstairs.

I walked inside—really mad at this point—and Ben and Tiffani were laughing but also felt bad about how mad I was.

Tiffani then helped clean up and helped Peyton put her clothes on. Then we all got in my car and took Tiffani and Peyton back to their house.

Ben and I went to my friend's house for a party and bragged about our recent foursome that my dad walked right into.

The next day my dad said to me in the car, "So is sex pretty rampant in high school?"

Inside The Adderall Empire
FRAGMENT SIX

Every day I swallow the pill, every time I enter the Adderall Empire, I feel like a phony. A lot of my friends may be angry at me for me saying this, but I think they are phonies, too. They are falsely forging themselves for temporary results.

And so am I. I lie to myself every time the pill touches my tongue and I gulp it down with a glass of water. We are all brittle souls wearing fake wigs, acting in the manner that society wants us to. Inside the Empire my personality is a smooth liar with a bad habit of not wanting to be itself.

I feel a merciless churn in my stomach when together with others inside the Empire. I find a connection that's synthetic and temporary on Adderall, mostly a plastic feeling.

Smoking weed and drinking with others is different. I don't feel the same way because it's not a matter of focus, like on Adderall, it's a matter of untying the shoes of ones imagination. And a conversation can go both ways.

On Adderall, it's "me me me." I've met so many people on Adderall who don't listen to your thoughts and only interrupt you with theirs. I think people do Adderall to get themselves to a different or better place, to impress someone, or accomplish something that they haven't done before. People don't drink alcohol and smoke weed to get farther in life; they are doing it socially.

But sitting around in a social circumstance taking Adderall, all you get is mind-numbness. If everyone was taking Adderall we would all be traveling robots walking around fooling each other.

That's why I wrote this book. People don't think Adderall is evil, they think it's heavenly.

CHAPTER ELEVEN

GRADUATION
Occurred: Spring 2009

The night before graduation was my friend William's 18th birthday and I invited him, Ben Johnson, and a few others over for a wild night. At this time I knew I had failed my physics class that day, but I felt I was invincible and most of all I was in denial. My buddies started to surge into my downstairs garage and we started drinking some Svedka that we had managed to swindle from a person twenty-one years of age. I didn't care about anything at the time except getting drunk. I was upset with myself for taking physics class when I could of taken P.E. Regardless I was a quarter of a credit short of graduating.

I had arranged to take the tests I needed to pass the next morning before graduation rehearsal, but that didn't stop me from pouring the Svedka down my throat. We were being a little loud downstairs in the garage and my dad walked in on William taking a gigantic pull from the Svedka.

"What's going on down here?" he asked.

I interjected and tried to handle this like a pro.

"We have graduation tomorrow so we are celebrating and its William's birthday as well. You can't be mad at us."

"What are you guys going to do tonight?"

"We want to go to the casino."

"Okay, well I'm not letting you drive, how about I call a cab for you?"

We all were shocked. We didn't know my dad could be so cool. If only he knew about what happened today in physics. Or did he? Well we were pumped on the thought of going to the casino so we proceeded to get nice and toasty drunk.

While at the casino I was getting all kinds of calls from my parents asking if everything was okay. Once I was in the bathroom with them on the phone asking me if everything was okay and I kept on saying, "Yes." I was totally lying because I was not going to graduate tomorrow unless I passed those darn tests. Eventually I broke down and told them.

Shortly thereafter we all caught a cab home and my friend Ben Johnson stayed up with me and tried to help me study, but we both knew it was pointless. I couldn't learn physics with a huge alcohol buzz.

The next morning I took off to school early to take the tests. My friends all knew about the physics fiasco so they were texting me notes along the lines of, "You got this man!" When I arrived at school I walked shamefully to Ms. Messi office. She said, "Do you know why I failed you?"

"Yeah, I copied off Shailene."

"I know. Everyone else was asking questions during the test and you didn't and then sure enough I noticed you were sitting next to Shailene and your tests were almost identical. Why did you do it?"

I felt guilty and realized it was so amateur-hour of me to copy a test identically. What was I thinking? Why did I do this? What's wrong with me? Now I'm not going to graduate high school.

"I, I knew I needed to pass this class to graduate and knew I was behind. All I need is a quarter of a credit. I'm an idiot. I'm so sorry. I understand and will take full responsibility."

"Look, here's what I'm going to do, I will let you take this test again and I will grade it and let's hope you pass, because I will feel horrible if you don't graduate because of this class. I can't believe you put me in this situation!"

"I know. I'm sorry."

She handed me the test and I walked out into the flex area and took it. It looked like it was a different language to me and I did not know any of the answers. I knew nothing. I was doomed. I filled out answers and scribbled botched answers when I had to solve a problem and show my work.

I turned it in to her about 9:30; graduation rehearsal was at 10:00. I was breathing heavy and my fingers were trembling. I knew I had failed, but thought maybe she would just pass me.

When she handed me back the test I saw the score in red pen with a circle around it: 27%. I failed. I dropped the test and put my hands in my face. Tears started to seep from my eyes. I took my hands off my face and looked at her.

"What do I do know? I'm not going to graduate!"

Then I took off out of the flex area into the hallway and started speed walking. I managed to get my phone out and texted William, Ben, and my mom, "I failed." I kept walking down the hallway faster and faster. I was mad at everything—mostly myself—and I kept walking until my phone started buzzing in my pocket.

A phone call?

"Hey mom," I mumbled with tears coming from my face.

"Go to the principal, she might be able to help you."

I mumbled back into the phone, "Love you."

My dad was on the line, too, and they both said, "Love you son, Love you."

I hightailed it to the principal's office to see Mrs. X. By that time she must have gotten a call from Ms. Messi, or maybe my parents. Who knows? Inside her office I was so upset and embarrassed. I thought I had failed high school. That was until she told me that my brother was on his way over with a work stub and that she was going to give me the quarter credit for community service.

I was going to graduate.

I couldn't believe it. There was no way. No Way. The crying was starting to diminish and I was somewhat happy, but still confused.

Then she proceeded to give me a lecture. It went something like this.

"Andrew, you can't live your life this way, cheating on a test in physics? Waiting until the last minute to address this situation? If you continue to go about your life living it this way, you will not get very far."

Everything else she said was a blur. I was thinking about so many other things and my mind was in a completely different place.

"Okay," I said. "I know I messed up. Sorry."

She escorted me out of her office and I ran outside and met my brother. I got the stub and ran it back into her office and she said okay, you can go to rehearsal.

"Thank you so much!"

I ran out of her office, down the hallway, down the stairs, and into the gym. It was 10:01. I made it. I did it. I was in shock.

My friends were just starting to get there and I told them everything that had happened. During the rehearsal all of my friends were hung over. William almost threw up; it was so funny watching him. I was hung over too, but I was high on life and was one happy camper. I was going to graduate high school. Wow.

———————

Later that day, when actual graduation was going to occur, some of my friends wanted to take Adderall. They thought it would give them rational thoughts and make them enjoy it more. I didn't care about anything anymore—I was about to graduate high school—so I gave it to them. About four of my friends took Adderall and another friend who has ADHD gave it to some his friends, too. There were about seven of us total who popped Adderall right before graduation.

We had about an hour before graduation when I walked to Seven Eleven with my friends Brody and Dino. We bought two Lokos with my fake ID. We walked to College Place Middle school and barehanded the Lokos, drinking them in public. We thought we were invisible because we were about to graduate high school. We cheered, smiled and laughed, and patted each other on the backs. It was majestic and nostalgic at the same time. One last Loko.

Then we hustled back to school, where people already had their robes on. We had to get a teacher to unlock a flex area to get our robes and then rushed down toward the football field. We made it. I remember right before we walked onto the field, we saw Ms. Messi in passing. She had no idea I was drunk on Loko. She came up and gave me a hug and was partly crying.

"I'm so glad you graduated and that it worked out!"

"Me too," I said back.

We all sat waiting for the ceremony to start, the sun beaming down on us. While all of us were on Adderall, we watched the service, whispering to each other the whole time. I wondered if anyone else took Adderall for this? Why had I given them Adderall? Do we really need to be taking Adderall for this?

I looked around seven pairs of glassy eyes looking outward toward the podium, searching for thoughts. Then more whispers of excitement. Friends pointed at the program, laughing with excitement. We had done it.

I remember shaking the principal's hand and running down the metal walkway of the podium, pumping my fists, high-fiving teachers along the way.

Then I remember sitting back down with my friends and buzzing off Adderall. What were we suppose to feel?

This is my brothers and me
after graduation from Edmonds
Woodway High School.

This is my family—Ron,
mom, me, dad, and Griffey —
after graduation.

Afterward we had an Escapade where all of the class of 2009 were going to stay up all night, some of us would get hypnotized, and then we would bowl, dance, and spend one last night with each other.

Was that why they wanted the Adderall? To stay up all night? For the life of me I do not know, but I know that they were taking it for all the wrong reasons, and so was I.

I think we all took it because it made us be someone we weren't and helped us give fake nostalgic responses to situations like gradation.

Now, looking back on all of this, I wonder if it was right for them to take Adderall and for me to supply it? I don't think it was a good thing for any of us because, at a moment such as graduation, one shouldn't need a pill to develop rational thoughts. Those thoughts should bloom in the moment.

Official Medical Record

July 23, 2009
Swedish Edmonds Birth and Family Clinic
21911 76th Ave. W., Suite 110, Edmonds, WA 98026

Andrew K Smith
Male DOB: 06/06/1990
Patient Profile: 19 Year Male
Height: 66.75 inches
Weight: 150 pounds
Pulse rate: 76/minute
Resp: 16 per minute
BP sitting: 122/76 (right arm)

History of Present Illness:
Here to follow-up ADD. Graduated high school. Will go to Arizona State in fall. Final high school GPA 2.6. States no problems with Adderall, allowed good focus. Taking this summer off, not working. Sleep good...Looking forward to college.

Impressions and Recommendations:
Review ADD treatment options, importance of organizational skills...Since out of state, he may need to see doctor at Student Health for refills. He will research options...If I will continue to prescribe, he will need follow-up visits at xmas holiday.

Official Medical Record

November 25, 2009
Swedish Edmonds Birth and Family Clinic
21911 76ᵗʰ Ave. W., Suite 110, Edmonds, WA 98026

Andrew K Smith
Male DOB: 06/06/1990
Patient Profile: 19 Year Male
Height: 66.75 inches
Weight: 151 pounds
Pulse rate: 80/minute
Resp: 16 per minute
BP sitting: 124/84 (right arm)

History of Present Illness:
Here for ADD follow-up. Freshman year at Arizona State. Had signed up for a lot of classes; some were too high level as he did not go to orientation. Had to drop a few classes that were too advanced. Has three classes. Doing well, has all B's. Adderall helping well with focus, using daily...Sleep good.

Impressions and Recommendations:
Review ADD treatment options, importance of organizational skills. Continue present prescription. Next follow-up six months.

Official Medical Record

December 21, 2009

Swedish Edmonds Birth and Family Clinic

21911 76ᵗʰ Ave. W., Suite 110, Edmonds, WA 98026

Andrew K Smith

Male DOB: 06/06/1990

Patient Profile: 19 Year Male

Height: 66.75 inches

Weight: 154 pounds

Pulse rate: 84/minute

Resp: 16 per minute

BP sitting: 126/80 (right arm)

History of Present Illness:

Here because he wants to do prescriptions online with mail pharmacy. Has new insurance and this is what is required...2.75 GPA first semester. Meds still doing well. Took prescription to Bartell's, states they did not give 90-day supply, but cannot say how much they dispensed. Patient or pharmacy did not notify this office regarding not filling prescription as written.

Impressions and Recommendations:

Call to pharmacy Bartell's. Pharmacist confirms only 30-day was filled. Advised patient that in the future please let us know if different amount than written is actually filled...New prescription written for 3-month supply for patient to send to mail away pharmacy.

Official Medical Record

June 28, 2010

Swedish Edmonds Birth and Family Clinic

21911 76th Ave. W., Suite 110, Edmonds, WA 98026

Andrew K Smith

Male DOB: 06/06/1990

Patient Profile: 20 Year Male

Height: 66.75 inches

Weight: 145 pounds

Pulse rate: 80/minute

Resp: 16 per minute

BP sitting: 116/84 (right arm)

History of Present Illness:

Here to follow up ADD. Just completed first year of college at Arizona State. Returning to Shoreline Community College next year. Grades: 2.83 GPA. Adderall works well for focus, helps organize studies…Sleep good… Has been running more in mornings…Looking for summer job.

Impressions and Recommendations:

Review ADD treatment options, importance of organizational skills. Next follow-up six months.

Official Medical Record

December 7, 2010

Swedish Edmonds Birth and Family Clinic

21911 76th Ave. W., Suite 110, Edmonds, WA 98026

Andrew K Smith

Male DOB: 06/06/1990

Patient Profile: 20 Year Male

Height: 66.75 inches

Weight: 143 pounds

Pulse rate: 76/minute

Resp: 14 per minute

BP sitting: 134/74 (right arm)

History of Present Illness:

Here for ADD follow-up. Got A in sociology class. Has not completed the other class yet, but doing well. Focus is good, organization is good. Three classes including math next quarter, which will be more of a challenge. Sleep is good.

Impressions and Recommendations:

Review ADD treatment options, importance of organizational skills. Continue present medication. Next follow-up, six months.

CHAPTER TWELVE

260 DIGITS

Occurred: Winter 2011

While I was attending Shoreline Community College I lived in the University District. One night, my bunkmate Riley and I came up with a crazy idea. I was going to try to get a girl's number every day for the rest of the month and write about it on my blog.

Day 1: 10 Digits 01/07/2011

I'm momentarily switching my blog posts up and am going to share encounters of me attempting to get chicks' digits. Every day, including today, for the rest of the month I pledge to get a landline or cell phone number of a female. (That's 26 numbers).

Let me tell you a little bit about today's number-getting experience. It was early morning in class and I was browsing around with my eyes, looking for a possible candidate. I landed on the girl sitting directly behind me.

She was cute and I had talked to her briefly the previous day during class, strictly miscellaneous talk. I wanted to get the number in the phone bank early so it wouldn't be on my conscience.

I made a few jokes about how the teacher was being repetitive and this made her giggle a few times during the period. Nearing the end I braced myself and waited for the clock to strike 9:30. A few seconds after it did, as everyone was gathering their things for departure, I spun to the right and said, "Any plans for the weekend?" She smiled and mentioned how she was a ski instructor and had to work Saturday and Sunday but Friday she was still trying to figure out. Then she flipped the question on me and I made up some random line and then asked her for her number. We made eye contact and she leaned in, creating a shadow over me. She told me her number in two sets of three and one of four. A total of ten digits. Thank you, Shannon. Day one accomplished. (206-794-08**).

Day 2

Feed me the rock and I'll put it through the hoop. Swoosh. Count it. Going to the locker room. Shower.

That is how I felt today during my number getting experience. I got off to a slow start and had no number coming into my second class. I knew that my second class had the most potential, though. I usually get there right before it starts so I only had a brief opportunity before I sat down to scour the room. I took advantage of this when I walked into the room. It felt like I was moving in slow motion when I entered the place. I ended up picking a third row seat next to a hottie.

I was pondering the entire class, trying to cook up a good entry. As the class ended I pushed some words out of my mouth. "Did you finish the homework for tonight yet?"

She replied, "I have ten problems left, not many."

Then I said, "The reason I'm asking is because I'm looking for someone to work on math with one of these days if you're down?" (It was all I had). I was so nervous at this point that I didn't understand a word she said but she had a big grin on her face so I slipped her the question. She gladly delivered it to me. It felt like I was floating when I put it in my phone. Why thank you, Kelly. (425-737-28**)

Day 3

Today I had the opportunity to go to the Seattle Seahawks playoff game and I took it. I ended up meeting some people who were a few of the coolest individuals I'd ever met. They were friends of my brother and we pre-funked it up at Fields, which is right across the street from Qwest Field. I was the youngest and shortest one in the place but I held my own. As the morning progressed, everyone got to drinking and we mingled like crazy. Before I knew it we were entering the stadium and I had plenty of choices to pick from girl-wise.

I passed on the first few batches but when the second quarter hit I went on a mission to the concourse for a number. It took me a good seven minutes to get into position. I ended up meeting a girl who was nearing the end of her holiday break and managed to snag her number. Then her mom showed up out of the blue. I was rattled and tried to make small talk with her mom as much as I could. It didn't last long before I meandered my way back to my seat with the digits in my phone and a grin on my face.

It was good to meet you, Mackenzie. (360-630-82**).

Day 3

After three successful days of getting girls' numbers I felt pretty confident that I would keep the streak alive. I figured Sunday would be my hardest day of the week and knew I had to be on top of my shit. I was on the hunt the entire day for a good-looking, proactive lady. The first stop was my school library and that didn't pan out at all. The next stop was the grocery store with my roomies. By the time we got there it was already 9:50 at night so I only had two hours and ten minutes to seal the deal.

I got my basket and began shopping around a little bit. I made a few trips all the way around the store, seeing what girls were there and trying to whittle down the prospects. One of the more attractive ones seemed a little older so I was a little timid to give her a shot. I'm glad I didn't because my roommate went and investigated her a little more closely and she was shopping for baby food so she was out of the race.

I finally showed up to the self checkout next to two babes who fit the description. Out of my peripherals I noticed they were beating me, and I wanted to finish checking out before them so I could pop off my line while they exited the store. Sure enough, I beat them and settled in my position. They began their exit from the store moving toward me. And keep in mind, not only was my roommate at the self-check watching me, but so was the checker, standing right there witnessing all this go down. Right as they crossed my path, I said, "Doing some last minute shopping?" They didn't stop at all. Instead, they continued walking and the shorter one said, "Yup," and exited the building. This caused the checker to break out a little laugh and say, "Had to give it a shot." All three of us laughed it off together for a moment more.

I got shut down tough today. It's the Sunday curse! Maybe I'll have more of a favorable outcome tomorrow.

Day 5

Maybe part of it is the fact that girls just seem to be getting more and more accessible. I mean, we have all these tools in today that provoke conversation. It just seems that these instruments are taking us away from the mysterious non-verbal things that happen in conversations.

Today I realized how much I've missed the pure, anxious feeling that I get inside my loins when I brew up some conversation from scratch. It was that sort of a tingle-like vibration that occurred today when I planted myself at that table in the library today. It was your run of the mill table occupied by a girl I had my eyes on for the length of time it took me to complete almost all my math homework. I kept taking my eyes off the screen and peaking at her. Then my friend warned me that the national championship football game was almost on so I blurted out to her, "I got a headache."

She didn't respond but I continued to look at her until, after a few moments, she acknowledged me and I pointed to the door. "I'm about to jet but it was nice sitting here with you even though we didn't talk at all."

She laughed so I rolled with it and talked about how her binder upkeep was better than my binder upkeep. It was the only material I had but managed to use it to my advantage and simultaneously opened my binder and slid it so it was facing her and asked for her number. Go me. Pencil me in for another successful day. Gracias, Kyra. (206-915-95**)

Day 6

I was limited on openings for using my skills so I had to do the impossible. Without warming up the conversation at all I went up to a girl as I was exiting the library today and said, "What's your number?"

She looked at me with the most confused and spooked-out look. I don't really blame her though. I mean, it couldn't have been a more random thing to do. But the library wasn't giving me as many chances as I imagined it would. I could tell she was trying to gather words to say something back, but before she had the chance, I said, "It's cool if you don't want to." We were both standing there uncomfortably, squirming.

I did both us of us a favor and resolved this forced, awkward, un-talkative situation. I figured I would say the funniest thing I could think of and run for the hills. So, as I was turning for the door to put both of us out of our misery, I said, "Smell ya later," and left. I never looked back. I wonder what the look on this poor girl's face must've been. Tomorrow I'm going to use other resources for getting numbers. But, if worse comes to worst, I can always ask randoms at the athenaeum again. I won't let all of you down again, I promise you.

Day 7

When I was strolling through campus today I saw a straight fox who was walking alone toward the parking lot. I made a beeline to catch her before she got to her car. I had to take bigger strides and speed up because, at the pace I was walking, I never would have caught her. There was a lot of slush throughout the campus today, so I was sliding around and losing my balance; it was quite the task. Finally I made it within a few steps of her and shouted, "Hey!"

She slowed down and turned around and then I said, "Are you new here?"

She replied, "No!"

I acted like I was interested. I nodded my head and said, "Well my friend's going to have a party this weekend, it should be pretty fun, you should come." She told me she was busy. I was desperate so I said, "In case you change your mind I can send you the address or something, just give me your number." She was pretty hesitant to give it to me but my persistence paid off and I got that number of hers. Thank you very much, Amber (206-384-86**).

Day 8

The fellas and I got together and went to Warm Gun's show tonight. We made a wrong turn on the way there, so we showed up mid-performance and meandered our way to the front row. Warm Gun was on stage and the crowd was into it; everything was going well. I was on my grind tonight and right away I spotted one of the cutest girls in the crowd. I consulted my friends and got approval. We were trying to figure out if she was really young or not. It was hard to tell because of the relaxed ambiance that was happening in the room. I couldn't keep my eyes off her, so I slowly but surely made my way next to her.

I pointed to the stage and told her I went to high school with Warm Gun. I still couldn't get a good read on this girl so I went along with the music and bobbed my head. Then Warm Gun finished up and "Mr.

Don't Give a Fuck" came on. Some random baby mammas and baby boppers started dancing in front of this girl and me. It was too funny for both of us to handle—we were both loving every minute of it. Then I asked her if she'd been here a while and she mumbled something that was hard to hear. So I kind of patted her forearm, and asked for her number.

You know when someone speeds up and you fall back into your seat? That's what she did, but standing; it was like a head check of some kind and she snatched the phone out of my hand and was putting the number in. While she was doing that I was giving the thumbs up to all my friends and doing the wiggly fingers. She was oblivious to this cheering. Finally she got her number in there and I bailed and told her I had to go the bathroom. We left shortly after that. If we were playing kickball, I'd pick you first, Makaela (425-530-58**).

Day 9

I was in the zone this afternoon in oceanography class. I got into a rhythm with the woman sitting next to me; every five or so minutes I would drop a random remark her way. Three remarks later I was in there like swimwear. It was only a matter of time before I asked for her cell phone number.

I was trying to figure out when the moment was right. I was over analyzing it in my head all throughout class. I strongly considered backing out. But I had put way too much time and effort into thinking about getting this girl's number so I couldn't back down now. Finally, I devised my usual scenario where I wait 'til the end of class and, as we were packing up our things, I would go in for the kill.

I've had a lot of success with this technique in previous days so there was really no reason for me not to keep doing it. I admit it was a little uncreative of me. Anyhow, I asked for her ten-digit code and she gave it to me. While this was happening I noticed the teacher was looking at this all go down. He had the biggest grin on his face and gave me a slight nod. So I did what anyone else in this situation would do; I looked in between the girl and the teacher and said, "Always good to have." Then walked out. Well played, Kimberly (206-999-97**).

This is Tucker Max and me at his book signing for "Assholes Finish First" in 2010 at UW.

Day 10

Oh what a day it was. I got off to a late start today but felt like I had the right recipe for success. The atmosphere was different from what I've been used to lately, so I knew I had to adjust. It was almost as if I were at the zoo or a safari park with everyone including me being all wild and animalistic.

The clock was ticking down, so I had to work fast. There was only one girl in my proximity who I didn't know at all so she was the only eligible nominee. After coming to this conclusion I grabbed my wing man and popped a squat next to her and sparked up a random conversation. I made the customary small chat with her and felt comfortable enough to go ahead and ask. It all worked out and she gave her number to me.

I instantly high-fived my friend and texted a friend to tell her about how I had pulled it out tonight. I think someone even tweeted about me saying "congrats Andrew."

The girl ended up going to her car to get something and that was a good time for me to move to a different location inside the venue. After I vacated to a new spot one of my friends who knew her told her about the blog. I'm not really sure how to describe that situation because I was in the middle of a game when she found out about it. I did get her number under verifiable circumstances before she found out about it though, so it still counts. Nice to meet you, Shannon (206-407-53**)

Day 11

If you're reading this, then it actually means I worked up the courage to post it, so good for me. There is no easy way for me to say this so I'll just say it: I didn't get a number today. It's a big bad world out there, stuffed with girls that hide inside in their bungalows rather than going out into the public. All I have to say is, "Good mother fucking choice."

On a more positive mark, I found myself doing a catcall outside the backseat window of my friend's car. It was projected toward a pedestrian walking on the sidewalk on 50th street. She gave me no response whatsoever. Yet somehow it was my best attempt at getting a number today. I'll have you know that I can't go back to the not-getting-number ways of the past though. I just won't. The third Sunday is the charm. Don't tax my gig so hard core cruster.

Day 12

All my good material came out this afternoon at the Teriyaki place. It really was a really good jump start to my week. I said one thing, she said another, and the next thing I knew, I had a number.

It started when I was in line waiting for my food and this girl walked in and placed an order. She ordered the chicken katsu and I had already ordered the chicken gyoza, so I couldn't use the classic, "Oh you got the chicken gyoza too?" speech.

So I patiently waited for my food and then talked about how this was my spot. She was very friendly and gave me good replies so I had a lot to work with. I was wishing I could camp out in the middle of the conversation for millenniums. This girl was the smart type, she could handle every one of my analogies. I really got into a rhythm when I was with this girl. I felt like a veteran quarterback, standing in the pocket, throwing first down after first down.

We ended up getting into the topic of bathrooms in public places and how some locations don't allow you to go to the bathroom unless you purchase something. We came to the conclusion that it was very European of America, because in Germany people have to pay to use the water closet. Eventually, my food was ready and, after I got it, I tucked it under my armpit and asked for her number. Nice to have met you, Meghan (425-345-69**)

Day 13

I heart women… I really do.

It was a monumental day. I climbed my way into double digits on a late night QFC run with some friends. Let me recap this for you.

After a few tours around the supermarket for a fresh batch of girls, I was feeling a little bleak. Nothing was going my way. So I sat down at a table in the front of the store near the self check-out line and waited for my friends to pick out some beverages. One of the two friends I was with finished up early and sat down with me. I updated him on the big goose egg I had on the board for the day.

We were waiting for our third friend to finish up when we saw two girls who were finishing up also. I told him I'd use my flirtatious zing by giving these two ladies a tender smile when they walked by. So as they were walking by I gave them a big smirk and one of them locked eyes with me, then looked away, then looked back again.

She gave me a soft wave and said, "Hi!" I unattractively mumbled back. I quickly reached the conclusion with my buddy that I should chase after them. So I scrambled out of my chair in a hurry, and bolted for the door. I was literally running after these girls and eventually caught up with them in the parking lot. I was trying not to laugh and asked them the most un-thought-out, blatantly obvious questions. Somehow, the Mr. Obvious out-of-breath approach worked, and one of them gave me her number. Enjoy your brownies, Diana (253-569-05**).

Day 14 (this is my favorite one)

Red Bull girls are a waste of time.

I was on the way back from hitting the links with my buddy and we stumbled across one of those promotional Red Bull cars. They are always driven by hot girls and, sure enough, when we caught up with the car on the freeway, two girls occupied it. I knew this was a good chance for me to get my number of the day but my exit was a half mile ahead. I was hoping they would take that exit too, but they didn't. So I had to improvise a little and I skipped my exit and told my friend sitting shotgun to get out paper and pen and write, "What's Your Number?"

My backpack was buried under the golf clubs in the back seat. He impressively dug out the pack in a quick manner and found some pre-calc homework that had no writing on the back of it. Then I got over into the carpool lane next to the girls. The pen I had was a ball point, so he had to scribble hard to make the letters stand out. Eventually I slowed down and tried to mimic their speed, so we'd be directly next to them. Soon enough, the Red Bull girls and us were right next to each other. My friend was putting the final touches on the note while we were both laughing so hard.

I was trying to act all serious and said, "Come on, focus." Then we would go right back to laughing our asses off. The note was finally ready and he pressed it up against the glass and kind of ducked. The laughing got even more intense. Then he lifted the note down and the girls in the car were laughing so hard and we were laughing so hard. It was one big laughing orgy.

Then the passenger put up five of her fingers. I was excited for a second, thinking that she was going to give me her number by using hand signals. I couldn't have been more wrong—the passenger was pointing to the ring on her finger, indicating that she was married. She gave me a smiling shrug. Then I slowed down and they flew down the freeway and got off at the next exit.

No number. Who knew that Red Bull girls were, in fact, married girls?

Day 15

A mental mindfuck can be nice when attempting to mindfuck yourself into going up to a girl. That's only half of it, though. Then you have to mindfuck yourself again to get yourself to ask for that girl's number.

Generating mindfucks on top of mindfucks, creating this cool process called mindfuckification.

I was in the Ray Howard Library today with my friend and it was beginning to get late. There were two girls in the very back of the library. My friend and I were more toward the center, but we could see them from our chairs. I was trying to figure out a good conversation starter and ended up coming up with the idea that I would ask if they had any spare colored pencils I could borrow.

I was still feeling reluctant about going up to them. I was listening to "Hollywood Hoes" by Wiz Khalifa and I mindfucked myself by saying that at the end of the song I was going to get out of my chair and walk over there. So two minutes and eleven seconds later I got out of my chair and went over there.

One of the girls was friendly enough to give me two colored pens and then I walked back over to my seat and used them for my oceanography homework. Then I dropped them back off and this is when I followed up. I managed to get off the topic of school and onto a topic of what they were doing that weekend. After that conversation went awry, I mindfucked myself by counting down from three. When I got to zero, I pushed the words out of my mouth and one of them filled my ears with numbers.

Mindfuckification anyone?

Thank you, Azra (206-779-08**)

Day 16

It was an extremely busy day for me, so there were limited openings for me to get a number. As the day progressed I managed to hook a fishy in the sea at a going-away party for one of my dear friends. This was a girl I had seen before, an acquaintance, but I'd never had a real conversation with her, so getting this number wasn't going to be the easiest thing for me. I casually talked to her here and there throughout the night, throwing in short quips.

It was fourth down for me and the time on the clock was about to expire so I had to make a play before it was too late. I was tired and wanted to go to bed soon, so I stepped up, and just straight-up asked her for it. She gave it to me. Thank you very much, Anastasia (425-773-20**).

Day 17
Goose Egg.

Days 18-24
In the wildest, busiest days of my life, I simply had no time to login or come into contact with the opposite sex. I wanted to finish this thing though, and I wanted to finish it strong and end it with a bang. Plus I know all of you reading this wanted to hear the sweet mellifluous sound of my enchanting chronicles.

So I was strolling along, doing my thing, when I was launched into a number heavy situation. It was like a guy's night met a girl's night when we got there. Yet the girl-to-guy ratio was colossal, so the probability was high for me. Not too soon after, I realized that most of the girls around me were dumber than shit, which instantaneously depleted my odds. Still, I landed on one girl who could maintain a conversation. I felt impenetrable, that nothing could touch me, I was soaring right into her tiny little heart.

All the while we were sitting in front of the fireplace, soaking up some rays. Then I popped the question for her number and had her put it in my phone. The number binge continues. Checkmate, Elizabeth (808-429-60**).

Day 25-26
It's done! No numbers the last few days. It was not quite the ending I had envisioned, but cut me some slack!

After twenty-six long days I've gotten a total of thirteen numbers. That's 130 digits, so halfway to my goal of 260 digits. I have to say the girls did come running at the swing of my bat, though. My batting average was a solid .500!

It's been an absolute blast. Special thanks go to my editor Riley, my good man Alex, and everyone else for their support. It's only a matter of time before I think of something else to do. Until then I'm passing my throne off.

Official Medical Record

May 23, 2011
Swedish Edmonds Birth and Family Clinic
21911 76th Ave. W., Suite 110, Edmonds, WA 98026

Andrew K Smith
Male DOB: 06/06/1990
Patient Profile: 20 Year Male
Height: 66.75 inches
Weight: 138 pounds
Pulse rate: 112/minute
Resp: 18 per minute
BP sitting: 124/82 (right arm)

History of Present Illness:
Here for ADD follow-up. Patient has continued on his stimulants, ongoing benefits. Medication is definitely helping with focus...However, his main concern with the Adderall is the extra cost to him. Two more weeks of school at community college. Admitted to Washington State University next year. Re-taking one math class, grades otherwise have been good...Has been running more, attributes weight loss to this. Sleep is good.

Impressions and Recommendations:
Review ADD treatment options, importance of organizational skills. He would like to try methylphenidate product. He will research with pharmacist which long-acting product will be least costly...He would then like to have regular release Ritalin on hand as well for weekends when he may sleep late or plans to consume alcohol in the evenings.

Official Medical Record

June 23, 2011

Swedish Edmonds Birth and Family Clinic

21911 76th Ave. W., Suite 110, Edmonds, WA 98026

Andrew K Smith

Male DOB: 06/06/1990

Patient Profile: 21 Year Male

Height: 66.75 inches

Weight: 138 pounds

Pulse rate: 90/minute

Resp: 18 per minute

BP sitting: 112/78 (right arm)

History of Present Illness:

Here to follow-up ADD...Patient "not really sure" about the new medication, does not help as much as Adderall, but is cheaper...A few hours after taking, did not notice benefit for concentration. Sleep has been fine...Will be working this summer doing landscaping, but not in school.

Impressions and Recommendations:

Review ADD treatment options, importance of organizational skills...He really liked the Adderall the best, so will try regular release twice a day... Patient thinks he will have no problem with twice-a-day dosing, in fact the flexibility appeals to him somewhat...Follow-up one month, prior to leaving for WSU.

CHAPTER THIRTEEN

JAIL

Occurred: Autumn 2011

I'm the worlds worst designated driver.

It all started last October when I drove to Seattle to see my University of Washington friends. We went to a house party and had a good time, but then left and decided to go to the new Ben's Drive-In restaurant in Edmonds. Everything was going according to order. Then the song "Till I Collapse" by Eminem came on and the car erupted with excitement. Being the kind driver that I am, I turned up the volume and everyone shouted the lyrics.

All of a sudden I lost control of the car going twenty-five and the car shook and wobbled and I was on top of a parked car. My adrenaline was going crazy and I did not know what to do. I asked everyone in the car if they were okay. Everyone responded that they were fine.

No air bags went off in the accident, which is odd. We all exited the vehicle and I called my parents and the neighbors called the cops, who were there within minutes. The cops interviewed all of my drunk friends and me. Shortly thereafter they took statements, read me my rights, and told me I was being arrested for reckless endangerment. They put me in the back of the cop car.

My parents arrived when I was still in the back of the cop car and they talked to me through the window. My mom was crying and my dad had a long face. Then my parents said they would give my friends rides home and told me to call them as soon as I could.

Every minute felt like a lifetime. The cop eventually got in the car and told me I was going to jail. I was so mad. I felt that I did not deserve this. I had injured nobody.

The cop took me to the hospital even though I insisted that I was not hurt. He said it was protocol. I had to walk through Swedish Hospital in handcuffs and waste a co-pay. He then took off my handcuffs and the nurse did little tests and told the cop I was fine.

The cop put the handcuffs back on me and we walked back to the car and he got on the freeway in pursuit of Snohomish county jail. I was scared for my life.

We arrived at the jail and he took me into a room where I had to strip off all my clothes and put on a blue uniform and orange crocks in front of some lady. Then I put all my possessions in a plastic bag and counted the cash I had on me. Twelve dollars. Before I could grasp what was going on I was escorted to a jail cell with eight other men. We were packed inside a small holding cell like a sold out game at Martin stadium.

Some of the men in the cell were stinky. Some were scary looking. Some were sleeping. I sat on the cement bench and waited. I was terrified. The air conditioning was blasting on us, which was some sort of torture technique, because everyone including me was freezing.

This was a game and I tried to figure out what was going on. There was one phone in the cell but I couldn't use it yet because I had not been processed or gotten a wristband with my number on it. I could not sleep. It was complete and utter torture.

Eventually they called my name and I went to get mug shots and fingerprints, after which they put me in a different holding cell. This is when I met a guy who was in the navy and he showed me how to use the phone. I had to have a private conversation with my parents in front of him. It was quite ironic to be telling my deepest, darkest secret on the phone while some stranger listened.

Hours later we all got word that we were going to be moved upstairs. Going upstairs is a good thing. A cop led us to an elevator and up a few floors, down a long hallway, through two securely locked doors, and into the real jail wear I was assigned a roommate, a bed, and toiletries.

I got to my room and made my bed and met my roommate: a total creep. Then I walked into the courtyard and grabbed a book and read for a little bit. The jail is two stories with cells in a big circle just like you see in the movies. There were crazy people in there yelling and people tweaking out.

Then I decided to get in line and call my parents to see if I made bail. I made it to the phone and called them and told them how scared I was. I wanted them to get me out of here. They said they went to post bail for me but the judge waved it because I have a clean record and I'm young and a good kid. But the judge wanted me to sweat it out a little bit and then I would be released.

I hung up and got mad because I really felt that I did not deserve this, but I was excited that judge waived my bail and knew I was a good person. Eventually I was released and walked out a door into some random street with a bag of my possessions. I met my parents at Starbucks.

Being in jail is one of the scariest things of all time. This is my deepest, darkest secret!

Official Medical Record

October 24, 2011

Swedish Edmonds Birth and Family Clinic

21911 76ᵗʰ Ave. W., Suite 110, Edmonds, WA 98026

Andrew K Smith

Male DOB: 06/06/1990

Patient Profile: 21 Year Male

Height: 66.75 inches

Weight: 136 pounds

Pulse rate: 80/minute

Resp: 12 per minute

BP sitting: 114/76 (right arm)

History of Present Illness:

Patient is here with mom. Had been feeling very depressed, lots of anxiety after moving to Pullman for school. Had suicidal thoughts, so saw doctor at WSU who started celexa and clonazepam about one month ago. Since started, has been feeling dizzy…Did not take celexa and clonazepam over the weekend because he was planning to drink. Still felt dizzy…Had some sleep disruption.

Due to medications, he had been avoiding social gatherings (where alcohol was available) at the advice of the doctor there, and this led to feeling even more isolated and alone.

Stressors: school, move to Pullman, planning for study abroad (Australia)…Depressed mood is better, no longer suicidal ideation, but still anxious.

Seeing counselor in Pullman…Had thoughts of wanting to "not be here," wishing was dead. Never plan. Thinks never would hurt himself because of his family, "it would not be fair." Still some passive death thoughts occasionally.

Impressions and Recommendations:

Review use of medications, recommended length of treatment, need to taper dose when discontinuing. Value of counseling, stress management and self care...Advised patient of side effects of both celexa and clonazepam... Advised him if side effects worsen to seek ER care promptly in between follow-ups there. Will set up follow-up with me as well over Thanksgiving weekend. No self harm contract discussed, and agreed upon. Continue counseling, recommended every week.

Official Medical Record

November 18, 2011

Swedish Edmonds Birth and Family Clinic

21911 76th Ave. W., Suite 110, Edmonds, WA 98026

Andrew K Smith

Male DOB: 06/06/1990

Patient Profile: 21 Year Male

Height: 66.75 inches

Weight: 134.4 pounds

Pulse rate: 102/minute

Resp: 24 per minute

BP sitting: 102/84 (right arm)

History of Present Illness:

Vertigo and right ear pain for eight days...He is dizzy, having difficulty thinking, is foggy...Things feel different, feels numb all over...Has difficulty explaining what is wrong and what he is feeling...Is on Adderall...Mom is here with him and states he is not acting himself...Not partying, not having a good time, off and wanted to sleep...He has finals but he is unable to focus to study for them. He is stressed about this.

Impressions and Recommendations:

Eustachian tube dysfunction. We will start a nasal steroid to help with symptoms...I am concerned about the dizziness and confusion...most likely due to his recent medications and changes...He is to hydrate and rest over the weekend...If he worsens, he will need to be seen sooner.

Official Medical Record

November 21, 2011
Swedish Edmonds Birth and Family Clinic
21911 76th Ave. W., Suite 110, Edmonds, WA 98026

Andrew K Smith
Male DOB: 06/06/1990
Patient Profile: 21 Year Male
Height: 66.75 inches
Weight: 131 pounds
Pulse rate: 86/minute
Resp: 12 per minute
BP sitting: 102/76 (right arm)

History of Present Illness:
Here to evaluate depression…Stopped the celexa last six days…Dizziness the same…Patient is still dizzy and "cannot think." Cannot describe it… feeling of spinning, unsteady on feet…Is not driving…Hard to talk because cannot think right…Struggling with classes…Feels numb all over…Right ear hurts at night…Vision seems blurry…He is understandably upset at the disruption in his ability to function, but is not dealing with the depression that was bothering him prior.

Impressions and Recommendations:
Either inner ear vs. neurological issue…I arranged an appointment on 11/23 with Dr. Howard to proceed more quickly with this evaluation as he is returning to Pullman next week. Trial meclizine, no driving.

Official Medical Record

November 25, 2011
Swedish Edmonds Birth and Family Clinic
21911 76th Ave. W., Suite 110, Edmonds, WA 98026

Andrew K Smith
Male DOB: 06/06/1990
Patient Profile: 21 Year Male
Height: 66.75 inches
Weight: 136 pounds
Pulse rate: 76/minute
Resp: 14 per minute
BP sitting: 130/90 (right arm)

History of Present Illness:
Here with both parents…Was seen by Dr. Howard on 11/23, had MRI that evening…was told there were two spots on his brain that could be either MS or migraine…Dr Zhou called later that night and was not certain of diagnosis, wanting to review films and have him seen again on Monday… Still has sense of foggy thinking, dizziness…Has NOT had any side effects of depression since going off the celexa and klonipin…Has not been able to do his homework…Parents just want him to feel good.

Impressions and Recommendations:
I have addressed many questions from both parents, very specific for possible diagnosis of MS…They have appointment with Dr. Howard on 11/28, then he plans to fly to Pullman.

CHAPTER FOURTEEN

STUDY ABOARD,
THE BOYS GO TO QUEENSTOWN

Occurred: Spring 2012

On a fine evening in late April I arrived at the international airport in Christchurch, New Zealand, on Easter Sunday. I had an infectious curiosity and my two buddies, Gary Roberts and Joe Benson. Joe was a hockey player from Minnesota who was majoring in business and gave up D1 hockey to study abroad. Gary was also a business finance major from Minnesota.

We walked off the plane and got through customs and expected an exotic nighttime because we had no prior accommodations. We assumed that we would just take a taxi into the city and then find a place to crash: improvise in style.

We soon found out from the taxi drivers outside that there was no nightlife in Christchurch and that we could book a spot to stay and get a shuttle. I was groaning because I did not want to do that. I was in denial that there was nothing to do in the city. Despite my lingering thoughts I decided to go to the info center and ask the lady, "What's the cheapest hotel here in Christchurch?" She told me the cheapest one was "The Airways Motel." She then made a few calls and I looked at my friend Gary with a big frown on my face.

Eventually, we caught a shuttle to the motel. When we got there the first thing on our list was to find food. We were told that a gas station open twenty-four hours was all that was open at the hour. We proceeded to buy 25$ NZ worth of food and beverage at the gas station for dinner.

The next morning we woke up and took the hotel shuttle back to the airport and walked to Jucy Rentals to find out if our van was ready for us to pick up. They informed us that it was not going to be ready until four that afternoon, so we paid, signed papers, and then took the local bus to Sumner, Christchurch.

On the bus we saw how the whole city was in shambles, devastated by the recent earthquake. This was something we had known about before we got there, but we did not know it was going to be this intense. Everything around us seemed gray and there was graffiti all over abandoned buildings.

When we arrived in Sumner, a local town inside Christchurch that held up a little better than Christchurch, there were some good coffee shops so we had a feast at Joe's Garage Cafe. This place had Bob Marley quotes in the bathroom and cool artwork of Pink Floyd on the walls. After we ate we walked through the city toward the swampy beach.

As we were walking along the beach we felt exuberated and excited about the adventure that was to come. We were all smiling, laughing, and taking pictures as the anticipation rose. Then the time came and we took the bus back to Jucy Rentals and got our van. We decided that Gary would be the best candidate for driving the roads. We were worried because it was the opposite side of the road for us.

That was when I realized that we might actually die on this trip. Thank goodness we bought the walk-way insurance so if we die our parents wouldn't have to pay a dime for the car damages.

When Gary pulled out of the lot and onto the open road my head began to go wild with thoughts and I was grabbing on the handle bar above the window with my eyes open wide. First stop was groceries, then a trip down Highway 1 to Lake Tekapo. We left the grocery store with our van stocked with snacks, along with three liters of alcohol from duty free and a 330 ml bottle of Absinthe. We felt like champions and we hit the road at seven that night for a little twilight travel session.

Gary had made a bunch of CD's with oldies music on them. Oldies was a genre I was not familiar with, but had always wanted to get into because there is so much history in the music. So his CDs allowed a fresh symphony of sound to funnel into my ears, making me tingle with joy.

We felt like we were leaving society behind as we pushed on the gas into the future. We prided ourselves on not being insulated from the landscape by glass windows and steel walls that you find on big tour busses. Our contact with nature was absolute and we could see more of the terrain and smell more of the countryside. At the end of the day we were saturated in fresh air rather than an air-conditioned hotel.

Gary sat to my right, driving, I was in the middle, Joe was on my left, and we were thirty-five kilometers from our desired location when we hit a patch of fog. This was one of the scariest moments of my life because I was tired, so my brain was not functioning at its full capabilities. This made me overly worried.

I looked to my left at Joe and he was crouched over with his hands pressing hard on his knees. I looked over to my right and saw Gary slouching over the steering wheel yelling, "I can hardly see, the brights only make it worse!"

Then, with a puzzled look on my face, I looked straight into the fog. Thoughts of death were becoming more and more relevant. I had thoughts of my funeral and thoughts of what a mess it would be when my parents saw our van crashed off the cliff. It was one of my darkest hours in New Zealand.

Thankfully, we ended up making it out of the foggy mess all in one piece. When we got to Lake Tekapo it was eleven at night and everything was closed. We did not want to get a fine for sleeping in public areas, but we could not find anything open, so we risked it and parked in a lot next to the Lake Tekapo Information Center. Before we slept we drank some of the duty free Jim Beam and shared some laughs. We couldn't wait 'til we got to Queenstown. The next morning we woke up early and realized that three grown men sharing a double bed, with one comforter, on a fifteen-day trip, was going to take some serious stamina.

The next day, as we continued along the open road and switched to Highway 79, we saw more of what we were traveling through because it was light out. The area was mountainous with the milky blue rivers, fresh bright skies, and puffy lambs. We had Eric Clapton turned up loud, our sunglasses on, and the colors of the landscape made me feel as if I was living in a postcard. At times during the trip I felt that we were modern day hippies drafting off the semis in front of us.

The road to Queenstown was narrow and this brought the fear back into my eyes. But this time it was mixed with a certain level of comfort because Gary seemed to have adjusted to the roads. We had now been going a hundred km per hour for quite some time with no issues, but at times my instincts would kick in and I'd think we were on the wrong side of the road.

I forced myself to accept the new culture, which required me to rationalize the situation and transformed me into a brand new person. I knew from this point on that I was going to have a whole new outlook on the world around me.

Finally we were starting to see the light at the end of the tunnel. We changed onto Highway 8 when we were in Cromwell. It felt amazing to have no personal phone, no computer, no connection with civilization. I felt free and that was something I had been searching for.

To this day, I feel that the trip changed me in some way. I knew that it was something I was going to carry with me forever.

We finally pulled into Queenstown with Bruch Springsteen playing on the radio. We were shouting out, "Beyahhhhh!" as the mountains kissed the water in a way that was so extraordinarily beautiful that it made me squirm. We had made it safely to our destination and now the only thing left for us to do was to find a place to sleep.

CHAPTER FIFTEEN

STUDY ABOARD, THE PRIVILEGE OF YOUTH

Occurred: Summer 2012

T he sun was beaming through the window of the car as I stared into the distance. Words began to form thoughts about the real meaning behind studying abroad. I began to realize that studying abroad is about the opportunities of youth and learning the actual value of looking somebody in the eyes and listening to other people when engaging in conversation with them.

Asking questions about people's lives is important and that importance is something I've grown to appreciate and understand. The actual studying itself is just the means to everything else. Being all the way across the world and learning life lessons is the big picture.

Then I turned my head to the right and yelled to the driver named Fadi, who is from Turkey, "I'm enjoying this mini trip to the sand dunes in Port Stephens." He looked at me in the rear view mirror and smiled and nodded at me. We were in a beat-up 1990 Toyota Camry, with no car insurance. The car was borrowed from another Turkish man named Rashida.

There were five of us in the car. The man in the passenger seat next to the driver was from Muscat, and I couldn't remember his name until the end of the trip when the other two people in the backseat addressed him as Salim.

It's interesting how I had an awesome time with Salim and didn't know his name until the end. The other two people with me were Joe Benson and Gary Roberts.

So it was me from the West Coast, Joe and Gary from the Midwest, and Fadi and Salim from the Middle East. All of us together were going on an epic adventure to escape the machine and the routines going on back at campus to travel deep into the semi-outback of Australia on a quest for sand boarding. We were singing our last anthem to our youth and our innocence was about to plummet.

"I'm putting on the Pink Floyd 'Wish You Were Here' album," yelled Gary. Everyone in the car began to holler and scream with excitement. I was a rookie on the oldies and didn't know Pink Floyd.

Next I grabbed Gary by the shoulder and, in a light voice, told him, "I've never listened to any Pink Floyd before. I don't even know what 'Wish You Were Here' even is?"

Gary laughed. "Dudeeee. You're in for a treat, we will listen to the whole thing, from start to finish."

Salim shouted, "Yes. You're going to love it man." Then Gary pressed the play button and it wasn't long before I realized that we were all on a magic carpet ride for the soul.

Lunch was approaching as we cruised the dry Australian pavement toward the sand dunes. Our hunger had grown so we stopped in New Castle, New South Wales, at an Aldi grocery store, and grabbed materials to make sandwiches. We hopped back in the car and headed to Port Stephens, New South Wales. All of us were passing around a bag of chips as we pulled into Port Stephens.

We parked the car and walked through the town looking for an info center for information on sand boarding. The city was small, so finding the info center was no big task. The five of us made our way into the information center and a older lady showed us on the map that the sand boarding was just across the way in Anna Bay. We thanked her and set out for Anna Bay.

A short time later we pulled into Anna Bay and there were camels and booths spread out all over to rent sand boards. The wind was fierce as we stood outside the rear of the car. We opened the trunk and made up some late lunch. The blazing wind made it tricky to eat our turkey, ham, cheese, and mayonnaise sandwiches. Then Fadi said, "God put the wind here in this beautiful spot to remind us that we must appreciate the land." This made the moment a bit more nostalgic and honest as we finished up our sandwiches. When we were all done Fadi said, "Take a picture of the trunk. It looks like a food cemetery." Joe and I busted out laughing.

Half laughing, I said, "We're stuck in a food coma."

After the food digested we made our way down the small hill where the camels and sand board tours were located. This was the first time Gary, Joe, and I had seen camels. We stood there and laughed, smiled, and tried to take it all in. These camels were soft, fluffy, and smelled like wet dog. Their kneecaps were incredible looking, and when the camel directly in front of me stood up, it was like watching a lawn chair unfold.

We wandered over to a military-looking booth and read in big letters: 'Sand Boarding Tours.' We approached the booth and I asked, "How much is it to sand board?"

A lady said, "25AU$ per person for the rest of the day. We close at four-thirty. This includes a ride out there." We turned and looked at each other and instantly accepted.

Shortly after we paid, our ride arrived and it was a US Military Hummer V8 diesel. This Hummer was slightly modified, with seats for all of us. It was amazing riding through the ponds and the steep hills in the dunes in this big beast. It felt as if we were in the middle of a desert as the engine roared loudly and we were propelled across the sand. At one point we saw a huge dune cliff and the driver started to speed up and yelled, "Hold on boys!"

We launched off the cliff, getting air, and landed vertical on the sand, still moving. It was an unreal experience bouncing up and down in that Hummer. After five minutes of plowing through the sand we made it to another location that had another booth with chairs, water, and white plastic sand boards for sale.

The guy waiting for us was a beauty. He taught us sand boarding and took some action photos of us well. At first, we were sitting down on the boards, using them as if they were sleds. Then we explained that we wanted to try them standing up so he took us to a separate location that was not as steep so we could practice until we were ready for the steep hills. He taught us where to put our feet and told us that we ought to be careful because people break their collar bones one these boards all the time.

Somehow I got volunteered to go first, so I hopped on the board and ripped down the sandy hill. It was rewarding flying down the hill in the wind with the cold sand beneath my toes. Standing at the bottom of the hill, I looked up at my four friends and thought about how four strangers all the way across the globe were getting along, hanging out, having a ball. But soon, I thought, we would all going to go our separate ways and head back to our previous lives.

Nonetheless Joe cruised down the hill, followed by Fadi, followed by Salim. But still no Gary. Gary remained at the top of the hill and all of us were shouting up to him, "Come on man, you can do this!"

That moment made me realize that my good friend Gary was a weenie. I just felt sorry for him because he was being so pathetic. All of a sudden he went for it but he stuck his hands deep in the sand as we went down the hill. This caused him to move slow like a grandma. He was excited as he went down the hill but I was mad that he didn't just go for it. Gary cheated himself, and it's something that he's been doing the whole time I've known him.

All of us were out there trying to enjoy one of the greatest adventures of all time and he was being reluctant. We drove three hours to escape life back at Macquarie University. There is nothing wrong with just letting lose. It's the privilege of youth. Someday when he is old he's going to realize it and that's sad.

My anger started to drift away and I began to soak up the good time. We drenched our feet in the sand and walked all over, looking for hills to board down. As the end of our time was nearing we saw a big hill and decided it would be perfect for our final run. This hill was extremely intimidating and Joe tried going down it first. He made it about half way before wiping out in the sand. Gary went at the same time but he went on his butt so he was still a weenie.

Then I went for it and, at the same time I heard Gary scream, "Wait, I'm going to record it!"

It was too late. I had already gone and I kept my balance and made it to the very bottom to a little swoop area where the hill meets the flat ground. I was going at such high speed that I lost my balance and hit my bum on the ground and got sand stuck in my underwear. All of us started to laugh at the bottom of the hill, when suddenly Fadi attempted to go down and he made it near the bottom as well but wiped out right before the swoop and tumbled. He was bleeding on his leg from the spill. He was a good sport about it though and he laughed at his fall.

Up next was Salim. We paused and watched as he went for it but he only made it halfway before he lost his balance and crashed. All of us stood at the bottom of the dunes with our hands on our knees—out of breath, our hearts content, with blood on our legs and sand in our ears. As we walked back to the Hummer I touched Salim on the shoulder and he smiled back at me, "I can't even begin to tell you how much fun this has been today," I said.

We all climbed into the Hummer and headed home, but we decided to get one last photo to remember this trip. So I set up a timer and got one with the sunset in the distance. Afterwards Joe came up to me and whispered in my ear, "We needed a fun time like this man. Did you have fun?"

I had a grin on my face as wide as the Grand Canyon and, half giggling, I said, "Yeah man, I had a blast. This is just what we needed." All of us got out of the Hummer and started to walk back to the car and I thought to myself, this is what the privilege of youth is all about!

Why does Gary have to be such a weenie?

Official Medical Record

July 25, 2012

Swedish Edmonds Birth and Family Clinic

21911 76th Ave. W., Suite 110, Edmonds, WA 98026

Andrew K Smith

Male DOB: 06/06/1990

Patient Profile: 22 Year Male

Height: 66.75 inches

Weight: 145 pounds

Pulse rate: 88/minute

Resp: 12 per minute

BP sitting: 130/86 (right arm)

History of Present Illness:

Here to follow-up ADD. Feels that Adderall is good dose, helps with focus. Has done well academically past semester...Sleep okay. Moods have been good. No more depression or anxiety. Feels that living overseas "fixed that."

Spent past semester in Australia, very good experience. Looking forward to returning to Pullman in August.

Follow-up neuritis—sometimes numbness in feet after running. Gets "whole body muscle spasms" that wake him up from sleep about once per week.

Impressions and Recommendations:

Review ADD treatment options, importance of organizational skills. Follow-up in Dec/Jan when back home on break.

PART IV

ESCAPING

Inside the Adderall Empire
FRAGMENT SEVEN

Days go by where I do not have a complete thought at all, and a rational one is an even rarer gift, a gift from the Gods. I think about the drought of thoughts through the years and how I have counteracted Adderall with alcohol, which has caused the drought continue.

Taking this drug helps and hurts you at the same time, but this is not a victim story. This drug is harming the ones who take it for years and harming the ones who surround them because they end up experimenting with it.

What has happened to my Adderall generation? We can no longer have a rational thought. Have people lost their souls when they take this drug? The phrase "Oh, I cant focus," is sad. Not only is it sad, it's false. People can focus if they try hard enough, but they just give up and choose not to, begging for a drug to help them. In some ways I feel bad because the way technology is rewiring our brains is making it harder for people to focus.

That's another thing that's so crazy. It seems like I am more creative because I have ADHD—always connecting things and trying to puzzle together different thoughts. Other people put together complete thoughts like butter, while I just keep on pulling the broken pieces of thoughts out of my backpack and putting them together, hoping they will surface into a thought here or there. Sometimes they surface into some pretty cool insights and I feel creative. Being crazy enough and optimistic enough to connect thoughts together: I think that is the centerfold of being creative.

Looking back on the all the bad things that I have done—from the streaking to the bridges I have burned in friendships, to the judge in Edmonds I disturbed—it all seems like a dream, a mirage. I feel so far away and so close to home at the same time. My eyes water, I hold back the tears. What do I do? Better yet, what have I done?

A realization lands in my consciousness: End of July I am surrendering Adderall and circling back to my wild roots. Time to trust my instincts.

I may become out of control and get myself into more trouble, but I have my college degree, so fuck it. I can't bare being on Adderall any longer. I am missing out on too many of the finer things in life.

Sure, I will seem like a weirdo to a lot of people, but at least I will be happy and, most importantly, honest with myself instead of being a slave to a pill. That's all I have to say about that.

Official Medical Record

June 18, 2013

Swedish Edmonds Birth and Family Clinic

21911 76th Ave. W., Suite 110, Edmonds, WA 98026

Andrew K Smith

Male DOB: 06/06/1990

Patient Profile: 23 Year Male

Height: 67.5 inches

Weight: 139 pounds

Pulse rate: 96/minute

Resp: 18 per minute

BP sitting: 110/84 (right arm)

ADHD Follow Up:

Not feeling anxious or depressed, no further panic…He wants to stop Adderall/stimulants. Reports that it really helps him focus, complete school work, pass classes and do well. However does not like the effect on his personality and creativity. It is his hope that since he will be done with school work in July, he will no longer need the medication.

Impressions and Recommendations:

If he continues to do well with this, may have routine follow-up in six months…

Plan:

1. The patient's medication will be until he completes class work in July, then patient to discontinue and observe how he does without stimulant…

CHAPTER SIXTEEN

OBSERVATIONS AFTER ADDERALL
Occurred: Summer 2013

Day One—Monday July 22nd, 2013

'm alive without Adderall gushing through my bloodstream. Every step I take feels heavier and requires more effort than before, but that's okay. My mind feels as if it's a big bag of jelly wobbling across the tiles of my house. Words are squirting everywhere in my mind.

Then comes the time to speak to a family friend who's staying at the house. I feel the words dribble off my tongue with nothing holding them back. There is no leash attached to my tongue now and it causes me to get lost in my sentences. I feel loopy. A run sounds nice, sweating out the leftover demons and resetting the hard drive of my brain.

Day Two—Tuesday July 23rd, 2013

I drove to the store today and felt clumsy when I walked through the aisles. I remembered where everything was located, but I felt a small pausing pulse that stopped me when I arrived at the produce area.

The oranges. I thought I'd make some fresh squeezed orange juice. It's summer, it's healthy, and why not? I couldn't help think of OJ Simpson and how he got his name OJ because the last drink he consumed before he went to jail was a glass of OJ.

My impulsive creativity is still in place but I feel this spooky excitement of the break up with the psycho bitch named Adderall. I didn't want to hear or talk to her again but I knew her chemical wounds were tattooed underneath the walls of my skin.

In the kitchen I attempted to describe where the butter brushes are and I paused and got stuck describing where that drawer was. I muttered a string of words and hoped our house guest could process them.

I sent some texts, which was much easier because instead of overthinking each text and doing several drafts in my head, I text with no filter. The pain of text messaging has diminished. My phone is not as scary as it used to be.

Day Three—Wednesday July 24th, 2013

Today I feel loopy and lost; my mind is sore and I didn't even drink last night. What's this? I have a kickball game in a little bit and I will have a few beers then—maybe my headache will go away or maybe it will get worse. I will have to be social, though, and play a super-intricate game. But not really. Oh man, now I just lost what I was saying.

All in all, I could say I feel like my thoughts are airplane windows and I can see comfortably and think well. There are several windows I'm bouncing from—one to the next—and it's creating this whirl of loops that has me discombobulated. My mind moves in lumpy circles and it's hard for me to put together thoughts that have substance. I know that will come soon, so I wait.

I went on a run today to try to get my thoughts in shape like the full moon that's approaching.

Day Four—Thursday July 25th, 2013

Today is Thursday and I feel more normal than I have since being off Adderall. My thoughts are less loopy and more complete. I gave running a go today and it helped me manufacture unblemished thinking, but I can see the wild thoughts that have entered my realm.

Yesterday at the kickball game I had to meet strangers who were subs for people who couldn't make the game. I found myself asking two girls a plethora of questions but not realizing the manners of my answers. I called one girl old.

We went to the Ravenna Ale House after the game and I created a huge discussion about tater-tots and how it's hard to find the right ones. Tater-tots either go over their crunch allotment and are super crunchy or don't have enough crunch and are super soggy.

Either way, let's see, next we drove over to Broadway and tried to get in Macklemore's music video. I was surround by a crowd of people breathing on my neck and I had a slight buzz going from the kickball game. I found myself trying to talk to everyone around me and joking around about the people who were climbing trees to get a better view. I envied them. I wanted to climb those trees like a marmoset.

My parents got back from vacation today and I made them a hero dinner with halibut and asparagus. I felt that cooking was a good way to calm me down. That's all I got for now—there will be actual rational thoughts that will sprout soon.

Day Five—Friday July 26th, 2013

My mind is not firing on all cylinders. Adderall was so marinated within my flesh that without it I feel empty.

I noticed that I'm more grumpy than usual and that's because I miss the Adderall but I feel this calm assurance that I'm free.

I feel loopy and it's hard to even drive on the freeway.

Day Six—Saturday July 27th, 2013

I'm at a wedding and I'm chatting it up like normal but I noticed that my alcohol tolerance is much lower. I feel the effects of drinking much more than I normally do. The remapping of my mind has begun—the battle continues to live Adderall free.

Also in the car ride to the wedding I noticed that I can't remember song lyrics as well as I had before and that bothers me.

Day Seven—Sunday July 28th, 2013

No writing.

Day Eight—Monday July 29th, 2013

I've crossed the one-week mark and I can now drive on the freeway without feeling loopy. I feel much stronger and more wholesome. But I have lost motivation to do things. I need my mind to reset and regenerate the crisp feeling inside my body.

Day Nine—Tuesday July 30th, 2013

I'm at an intersection wondering where I'm about to go—just waiting for the light to change to green. Have I been insane all along? Was Adderall the cure? Is there no cure for the insane? My thoughts move from the verbs I pronounce.

Day Ten—Wednesday July 31st 2013

Every day gets easier being without Adderall, and I feel that I have made it over the hump. At the same time I broke down and called in a prescription for Adderall. It's ready to be claimed at Birth and Family Clinic before dropping it off at Bartell's.

Do I dare go get the prescription and take the easy way out? Do I dare re-enter the Adderall Empire? What does this say about me? Have I done anything wrong yet? I haven't taken the pill yet but my mind wants me too and my body doesn't.

Will I go fill the prescription tomorrow and will I take it? Maybe I'll just stare at it and look deep into the pills and see the memories we made together—I'll say goodbye again and touch the orange plastic crust on my fingertips for one last goodbye. I miss the psycho bitch named Adderall and I feel lost without her.

PART V

THE ROAD TRIP RELAPSE

CHAPTER SEVENTEEN

ADDERALL DREAMER

Occurred: Late Summer 2013

After two weeks sober from Adderall—fully clean from the stimulant—I relapsed while driving down Pacific Coast Highway 101.

My friend George Mazzerati and I were trying to find happiness from our worrisome shells. We cruised down the road—two mad men pushing the little pixies through the wasteland that sits below, where the black sleek wheels full of bouncy air watch out for the twirling and swirling dust-devil radar enforcement. The coastline of blue safari ripples with out-of-bounds smells with no sleep because we know time like Sal Paradise and Dean Moriarty.

We were looking for a place to stop and drink near pits of the road and we kept on spurting to a halt since society labels all the prohibited places along the treks of the pacific coast highway. Finally we rumbled onto some gravel near a logging site and then falsely suspected a human hand in the site so we scrambled out of there faster than bank robbers.

We were alive.

Nighttime was approaching as we cruised down the highway. This is when I had an Adderall dream that gave me an astonishing insight into the disfunctionality of my relationships with women.

George is one of those drivers who jerks all the time here and there. It's a real thing, and it causes me to grab my "oh shit handle" all the time. Anyhow, while passing cars on the highway I was drifting off into a nap and the car jerked. I awoke from my dream. We were heading east of LA to Indian Wells, and all of the sudden my head jolted up and I said, "Whoa, just had an Adderall dream."

He said, "Oh yeah, I know those, they always have crazy realistic worlds."

Then I started to tell him about my dream and how it gave me the most reflective insight about my life. Mazzerati was both baffled and impressed.

"Mazzerati! I figured something out in my dream."

"What is it that you figured out?"

"Every time I meet a girl I use this 'tool kit,' this usual procedure. I follow a series of steps and give a series of pre-used scripts that I have memorized that show high success ratings."

"Tell me more about this script you use."

I scratched my head, "Okay, I'm not really being me, though, just as Adderall is synthetic my relationship with that girl is, too."

George takes a puff from his cancer stick.

"It's like she doesn't even know who I am, I'm just this persona that I've built brick by brick, that I originally created to sleep with girls."

"I'm stunned you just realized this now!"

"Me too. They are also just using this persona that they've created to get guys to like them and sleep with them!"

"What don't you like about it if you do the same thing as the women do?"

"Well, I don't like the falseness of it, and that the fishing line I'm casting is only reeling in a very specific type of girl and a relationship."

"Well, what are you looking for?"

"I guess I would like to have a girlfriend—these girls are not the right breed for me."

"Do you think you're looking for love—to fall in love and be loved by a girl in return, but be loved for who you actually are, not the fake persona you use to reel them in?"

"Dudeee," I said. "Yeah, I'm looking for love."

We both laughed a little and then I asked, "How do I get past the false and pretentious walls that both of us are putting up against each other?"

This is when I realized that if I somehow could break down the barriers a girl and I both deploy that we could actually commit to one another for who we are. That's just it, and that's what my dream granted me insight into. It was something that I had never fully wrapped my head around.

The dream gave me awareness of several things: what it is I'm doing each time I pursue a girl, what it is they're doing, and how it's just the same thing. It also showed me how this has determined the girls I've been with and explained how synthetic my relationships have been. Lastly, I realized that I don't want the results that I have been getting.

George ashed his bud in the ashtray inside the car below the radio deck.

"How does one find love? What is it when you have it and how do you know it?" I asked.

"Well if it's love you're after, your tool kit will not suffice."

"I'm so used to the toolkit though."

"I think it's actually counter productive to your goal because is important in falling in love is that you guys are intrigued by the person you actually are, not the false persona."

"Yeah, that false persona man, it's gone on too long."

"You guys have to know each other truthfully and trustingly."

I nodded in agreement, partly smiling.

"In turn loving what you learn about the other person, even the weirdest or most vulnerable things about them."

Then Mazzerati dropped the Hank Moody line on me from Californication.

"You not only have to physically be naked with these girls, but you have to figuratively and mentally be naked with them." He laughs. "You guys must be able to be 'exposed to the elements' in both ways to really have a relationship that's worth while."

"Well actually finding a girl in this way, what does it take? Because all I can seem to do is use the toolkit method."

"Look I am hopeful in my own method. It doesn't get me laid but then again it doesn't drown me in meaningless pussy when I would rather have something worth much more."

I was frustrated, but I had to give it to him. He was right.

Then he said, "I told you how I always try to act, which is to act like myself. I first get in touch with who I am, what I believe, and who I want to be. Then I act in accordance with this. The more you get in touch with these things about yourself, the more you can act purely. That's what I think has the best odds of reeling in the kind of girl you're looking for and one who you can have a meaningful relationship with."

What Mazzerati meant was that I should reel in with the tool kit and then try to segue into deeper conversations with the girl—figuring out what it is they really want on this planet, how they feel about different topics, what their goals are, and I should reciprocate by sharing these things with her. He would call this being intellectually intimate rather than sexually intimate.

"This will be a hard transition for me to undergo, man."

"I know, but who knows, many of the girls you reel in with your tool kit may in fact have been perfect for you but you never really explored their minds, just their bodies."

We both laughed and zoomed off into the dark sky with a new feeling inside our bones. We were hopeful that these intellectually stimulating girls might be out there.

CHAPTER EIGHTEEN

INDIAN WELLS

Occurred: Late Summer 2013

The view was majestic with dim greens that tarnished the landscape. A few million acres of land made my eyes dance inside my skull. The Toyota Corolla roared and bumped down the highway over worn potholes, taking us deeper into the desert. There were small, deforested pockets, burned and scarred from forest fires. It was a traveler's paradise, a wasteland of overheat; the community thrived off of the heat. Mazzerati reached in the middle console, pulled out a fresh cigarette, and plopped it in his mouth. He borrowed a lighter from me, bent down and cupped his hands, and lit it.

The next morning we awoke and traveled to my house in Indian Wells, CA, where the weather is hot and the town is quiet. Mazzerati is in his early twenties and I've known him since I've known anybody. There are pictures of us on the mantle—young and resilient with our baseball caps on our heads.

Even as college wore on, when we had less and less to say to each other, we were still tied by a knot. We were stuck with each other, our attics full of old memories. His hair was short and red. He has the personality of a king salmon, always swimming to my rescue as the leader and unwilling to sacrifice his beliefs for his own satisfaction. He is brutally honest no matter the outcome.

The next night we were drinking some cold Bud Lights out of the can and moved outside to smoke a cigarette and talk about life. He swirled the beer can in one hand and took a puff from the Camel Filter in the other. I stood there gripping my beer with my smoke at my side.

"Try to ash it in the can," I said.

He nodded.

"You know," I said, "you, Jeremy, and William are the smartest friends I know. I wish I was as smart as you guys."

"Look, there is an intrinsic nature of society that attempts to grasp this notion of normal—"

I interject, "Carry on."

"Anything that deviates from this norm is then of course considered abnormal."

"Okay," I said.

He took another puff and exhaled. "Through its many mechanism THE SOCIETY either shuns the abnormal, or wraps its incredible might around them to reshape them in the likeness of its accepted norms."

"What are you trying to say, man? Continue though. I'm intrigued."

"There are some, like you Andrew, who grow up and have no idea what this process of social mechanisms is doing to you for a long time."

"This sounds like me. Okay."

"You can tell that something is pressing up against you, that somehow you're not like everyone else, but can't put your finger on it, which then causes you to unconsciously act out in even more aggressive ways, even more obnoxious ways."

I nodded, still intrigued about what he was saying, trying to digest the sentence.

"Then you suffer from consequences, which then makes you desperate to try any solution you can that society has to offer for your so called disorder. Not your fault, that's just how it is. What you realized after enduring that bull shit for years and years is 'well, wait a minute what the hell am I doing this for?'"

"So this is where I wonder why they are giving this treatment, the Adderall?"

"Yes, you have told me multiple times you don't even know who you are anymore." He paused. "Look, many never really take the time and effort to do such a reflection on what's going on with them and around them."

"Really?" I said.

"Many just fall in line without knowing, they just live and try and do so in the specific way they're SUPPOSE TO LIVE."

I stood there and took a drag from my smoke and looked up at the sky and thought about what he said. Then he kept going. He was in the zone.

"But there are also many who do take the time and effort to see what's really happening around them."

"What do they see?" I asked.

"They see differences not as an abnormality but as an inevitable fact of human life."

"What do they understand?"

"They understand what behavior will help them succeed and what behavior won't help them, or what behavior is not worth their time to explore."

"Wait so what about William and Jeremy?"

"These guys are the ones who recognize completely what is happening around them."

"Meaning what? They recognize this and do nothing about it?"

"When it comes to socially proper behavior, even if they feel that a certain behavior or action is foolish, immoral, or against what they actually believe in, they will refuse to act based on their own justification, and instead they will act the way that will bring them the most social gratification."

"Wait, so they know this but decide to keep doing it?"

"Yes, they even know sometimes that this is what they're doing but don't care, they care only for their own happiness, and this behavior gives it."

"They think that standing up or confronting their own misconduct is a waste, that they are powerless to change the flow of the current. Understandably, too. It's not easy to be a single fish swimming along with all the others and say, 'Hey this is wrong I'm going against the current.' They will in be trampled by all the others swimming. These people, if not checked by someone, or sometimes by themselves, will even convince themselves that the socially acceptable beliefs are their own, that they choose this persona."

"William and Jeremy sacrifice their beliefs, they choose not to stand up as leaders to direct the fish swimming in the river to the right paths and instead follow in line. What they don't understand is that if all the people like them stood up to this, there would be enough to change the flow of the fish. They also don't see or don't care to see that every time that they stand against the social machine they put a dent in it. Plus, they might even give someone else the courage to do the same. Then that person brings someone with them and exponentially this rebellion to the status quo grows and the chance to actually make a real difference for the greater good grows as well."

So how does this relates to me?

I am looked at as not as smart as George, Jeremy, and William in society. But society is looking through a restricted lens, from one set of rules about the world. This lens and these rules even has me believing that I'm not as smart. But underneath it all, we all have intelligence and desirable qualities, and we all lack something. No one human has it all.

Inside the Adderall Empire
FRAGMENT EIGHT

The Empire inhabits me and tears me to pieces. People may choose to come in, but it's the lazy way to succeed. It's a bad habit and I will be fully off Adderall. That's a promise.

I couldn't tell if that was a rant or good.

CHAPTER NINETEEN

LUMOSITY

Occurred: Autumn 2013

———————————

I sit at my desk and watch the bottle full of orange capsules next to my computer screen. I could take the pill that requires no work at all. I could swallow it and boom, I'm focused. Or I could go online to Lumosity and do my favorite exercise memory matrix to work out my brain muscles.

This requires lots of effort but has greater dividends in the long run. I've seen it before in the Cogmed Clubhouse. But Cogmed costs over two thousand dollars and Lumosity is around eighty dollars a year.

I think I'll choose the cheaper route.

I lean back in my chair and think harder while looking at my computer towering over the little cylinder pill bottle. They are side by side, my past and my future. I know that I want to be the real me and I want my wife to meet the real me, not the synthetic version. And so I know deep down in the reds of my heart that I will continue to challenge myself with the online exercises of Lumosity.

I will escape the synthetic man I have molded myself into throughout the years. Then I can be true again and happiness will bloom within my soul and I will be the person I was before Adderall, but with a stronger sense of right and wrong.

Sure, I might offend someone here and there by something inappropriate at the dinner table, but, one day, when the Lumosity takes full effect, those dinner table embarrassments will disappear. Even if they don't, at least I will be free of the Empire.

I look back on the endless string of trouble and wonder. I wonder about all the people who think they have ADHD—and in some ways we all do—and I wonder, do they really need a pill?

I don't think so, I don't think I need a pill either.

The obstacle is that the world is one big zoo of gushing details, impressions, and distractions. Very often I'm unable to unpack or string together any order or priorities. Keeping one thought in my skull long enough to act on it is not always possible. I manage to lose myself in the jumble of details.

———————

I am an optimistic man weaving these thought puzzles together. Some puzzles are not for everybody, and some things make sense and stick. What I have is these words; that's one thing both me and others have.

So here I am, a scientist of words, or maybe a father of words, impregnating my brain with words, making thought babies here and there. Sometimes those thought babies develop into real, fully-bloomed human thoughts, and sometimes they die in the womb of my brain. I am impregnating my brain with words making thought babies—hoping the thought babies grow into rational thoughts, into mature adults. But sometimes I am just demolishing a hole into forevermore with no thought babies surfacing. Sometimes I don't have enough in the tank to make a baby. The semen of my mind is flooded with these drugs, trying to make thoughts, and maybe the drugs help.

But on Lumosity I felt that it was possible for me to have a place in the modern world without Adderall. And when on 'The Front 9' of life, one shouldn't need a pill to contain his true self—otherwise how is one going to find his identity?

ANDREW K. SMITH

Andrew K. Smith at Yost Park

Andrew K. Smith is a Pacific Northwest native through and through. He grew up in Edmonds, Washington, but spent his undergraduate years across the mountains at Washington State University studying English and Creative Writing. The literary and arts journal LandEscapes published both his fiction and nonfiction work there, and in 2013 he received an honorable mention for the Sarah Weems Award in creative nonfiction for an essay-length version of *The Adderall Empire*.

Andrew worked part-time as a writer for Camp Korey, a summer camp for children with life-altering medical conditions. He enjoys reading on Sunset Avenue in his hometown of Edmonds, Washington while watching the sun set over the Olympic Mountains. When he's not in his hometown he's huddled in a coffee shop in Seattle collecting words.

www.andrewksmith.tv
www.theadderallempire.com

CPSIA information can be obtained at www.ICGtesting.com
Printed in the USA
LVOW10*1756220614

391147LV00017B/449/P